"Neat book...Really great job."

~Steve Dunn
AM Northwest, KATU-TV
Portland

"GRRREAT reading for all kids and their families."

~Yvonne McMillan
Interpretive Ranger
Lava Beds National Monument

"Thoroughly 'kid friendly' guide book..... Very highly recommended for any family planning to visit these west coast parklands."

~Margaret's Bookshelf
The Midwest Book Review

"This kids' eye view of natural history will make your visit to the national parks even more enjoyable. It's packed with facts about geology, plants, and animals, as well as environmental and resource management issues. Science, history, and fun all rolled into one — the perfect package for family members of all ages. I loved it!"

~David Peterson
Research Biologist
USGS Forest and Rangeland
Ecosystem Science Center

"This book will help kids have fun in parks, and learn something about preserving our national parks and the natural world."

~Kathy Tonnessen
Rocky Mountain Research Coordinator
National Park Service

"Thank you, Laura and Jenna, for writing next year's perfect Christmas gift."

~Tonnie Maniero
Biologist
National Park Service

"A treat to read for young and old, this book is filled with information about the parks and many wonderful adventures."

~Gary Larson
Aquatic Ecologist
USGS Forest and Rangeland
Ecosystem Science Center

"Their style of description is informative, entertaining, and, above all, perceptive... The Sullivans put together an interesting and insightful presentation of the park [Lava Beds]. *Surprisingly, on their first visit, the writers discovered and wrote about some of the parks' secrets that even many locals don't know about."*

~ Sean Nelson
Teen Correspondent
Klamath Falls Herald and News

*"***** So good it's hard to believe it's written by kids."*

~ Michele Hernandez
Top 100 Reviewer for Amazon.com

"The young authors approached the subject of the parks....through the eyes and ears of a scientist."

~ Laurie Kavenaugh
Enterprise Record
Chico, California

Kids' Guide to the National Parks of California and Oregon

Written by Kids for Kids*

Jenna M. Sullivan
Laura C. Sullivan

*but parents might learn something too

E&S Geographic and Information Services, Corvallis, Oregon

Kids' Guide to the National Parks of California and Oregon
Written by Kids for Kids

E&S Geographic and Information Services
P.O. Box 609
Corvallis, OR 97339 USA

Copyright © 2001 by E&S Geographic and Information Services

Printed in the United States of America
Second printing, August, 2001

Publisher's Cataloging-in-Publication
(Provided by Quality Books, Inc.)

Sullivan, Jenna M.
      Kids' guide to the national parks of California and Oregon : written by kids for kids* : *but parents might learn something too / Jenna M. Sullivan, Laura C. Sullivan. -- 1st ed.
      p. cm.
      Includes index.
      LCCN 00-107975
      ISBN 1-880062-23-2

      1. National parks and reserves--California--Guidebooks. 2. National parks and reserves--Oregon--Guidebooks. 3. California-Guidebooks. 4. Oregon--Guidebooks. I. Sullivan, Laura C. II. Title

F859.3.S85 2001   917.9404'54
                                          QBI00-901464

Table of Contents

Page

Acknowledgements...7
Introduction..9
Redwood National Park...15
Yosemite National Park...25
Sequoia and Kings Canyon National Parks.................47
Pinnacles National Monument.....................................61
Point Reyes National Seashore....................................69
Lassen Volcanic National Park....................................77
Lava Beds National Monument...................................89
Crater Lake National Park...103
Conclusion...111
Index..113
About the Authors...116

Color Plates
    Plate 1. Fern Canyon, Redwood National Park
    Plate 2. Yosemite Falls, Yosemite National Park
    Plate 3. Fern Cave, Lava Beds National Monument
    Plate 4. Crater Lake, Crater Lake National Park

This book is dedicated with love to Grammie, the intrepid traveler, on the occasion of her 90th birthday.

ACKNOWLEDGMENTS

We would like to thank our parents for helping us immensely with the making of this book. We never could have done it without them.

We want to thank the many Park Service people who were kind enough to grant us interviews, provide us with information on the national parks, and give us lots of insights into what the parks are like. These include Leonel Arguello, Loren Berlin, Kitty Borden, Kathy Carlise, Craig Dorman, Annie Esperanza, Dick Ewart, Gary Larson, Yvonne McMillan, Tonnie Maniero and Chad Moore. Lee Stetson, an actor who portrays John Muir, kindly gave us his insights on the "Father of our national park system." We also wish to thank Susan Binder, Jayne Charles, and Kai Snyder for their help in putting this book together.

Judy Rocchio and Bruce Nash helped us to get four photographs from the National Park Service that we included in the book. The Sierra Club kindly allowed us to use a photograph of a painting of John Muir from their website.

We would also like to thank the many scientists and people from the Park Service who gave their comments, insights, and suggestions on our book in draft form. These people include: Dr. Kathy Tonnessen, Yvonne McMillan, Dr. David Peterson, Curtis Doucette, Tonnie Maniero, Bill Shook, Chad Moore, Dr. Gary Larson, Leonel Arguello, Annie Esperanza, P. Deborah Sullivan, and Dr. Timothy Sullivan.

CREDITS

Desktop Publishing:	Susan Binder, Deian Moore
Cover Design:	Susan Binder, Deian Moore
Illustrations:	Jenna M. Sullivan
	Laura C. Sullivan
Photographs:	Laura C. Sullivan,
	Jenna M. Sullivan,
	P. Deborah Sullivan,
	Timothy J. Sullivan

Introduction

"You must not know too much, or be too precise or scientific about birds and trees and flowers and water craft; a certain free margin, and even vagueness-perhaps ignorance, credulity- helps your enjoyment of these things."

~ *Walt Whitman*

Are you ready to experience the trip of a lifetime? Then read on! Last summer, our family took the most amazing journey. We explored nine of the national parks and monuments in California and Oregon. Our dad is a scientist whose job was to visit the national parks and write a report to summarize the resources that can be damaged by air pollution. He had to go to each park, meet with park scientists, and get information for the report that he was writing for the National Park Service. We, as kids, begged to come along and made lots of promises about how we could help by photocopying research documents for him. Little did we know how much photocopying he had in mind! ☹ He finally agreed to take us along, and so on May 29th, the four of us (Mom, Dad, Jenna and Laura) set off down the coast of Oregon. This marked the beginning of our exciting journey.

Over the next four-and-a-half weeks, we explored forests of towering giants, stood next to raging waterfalls, swam in ice-cold waters, hiked up mountain valleys, discovered mysterious underground caves, viewed many spectacular wildlife species, and even managed to talk Dad into a quick detour to Disneyland. We ate strawberries the size of our fists, toured the incomparable Hearst Castle, and saw the biggest concentration of geothermal features west of Yellowstone National Park. True to our promise, we did manage a lot of work for our dad, but we still had plenty of time to explore the majesty of some of the finest national parks in the world.

Because we couldn't find much in the way of books for kids our age on exploring the national parks, we decided to write one of our own. We thought it would be a good idea to write a book telling kids like us the best spots and things to do if their parents decide to go on a trip like we did. To get much of our information, we also did research on the trip. In most of the parks, we found a knowledgeable park ranger or scientist to interview, plus we both kept detailed journals of our trip and collected fliers, books, and publications to serve as source materials. We tried to summarize our favorite spots for this book, and the things most interesting for kids to do.

This book has a primary focus on science and nature. There are several reasons for this. The first and foremost is that many of the national parks were created because they had some special scientific value. For example, Lassen Volcanic was preserved for its amazing geological features; Redwood and Sequoia to preserve their huge trees; Pinnacles National Monument to protect its interesting rock formations. For each park there was a scientific reason to have it set aside. National parks also provide wildlife refuges and places where plant and animal species can hang out without being disturbed. They are also extremely important for preserving biodiversity. Because science was the main reason many parks were formed in the first place, we thought it would be a good idea for you to learn about that scientific background in your travels. Another reason we chose to focus on science

Mylitta Crescent

Laura Sullivan

and nature in our book is because we like it. Our parents are both scientists, and therefore we have learned a lot about science from them.

Now we will give you an outline of our trip. We left from our hometown, Corvallis, Oregon. Our first stop was at Harris Beach State Park, where we spent the night. It was a pretty park with a nice view of the beautiful Oregon coast. The next day we traveled down to Redwood National Park where we stayed for three days before moving on to Yosemite. From Yosemite we went to Sequoia and Kings Canyon National Parks. These parks are next-door neighbors, so they can be visited as one. Then we moved on to Disneyland. Even though this is not technically a national park, it is clearly of national importance, especially to kids. That was good enough for us to make it a stop on our journey! ☺ After two fun-filled days with Mickey and Minnie, we regretfully headed north. We made a three-hour stop in Santa Barbara, where we went swimming in the ocean and rode a pedalina (a bicycle built for four). On the way to Pinnacles National Monument, we decided to take a detour to the Hearst Castle at San Simeon. It was a stop we wouldn't miss, and when we took the tour we were all awed by the magnificence and the grand scale of the castle. The only bad parts of the tour were that we didn't get to see the whole place, and they wouldn't let us swim in the pools.

From San Simeon, we drove up the coast of Big Sur and over the Santa Lucia Mountains to our original destination, Pinnacles National Monument. On the way, there were places where the edge of the road plunged down for several thousand feet. It was scary, and during the bad parts there was a particular noise coming from our mother's area. Sometimes it resembled a shriek, but later she assured us it wasn't. After Pinnacles, we traveled up to Monterey and Carmel, where we saw many California missions. We especially liked the Carmel Mission, Santa Barbara Mission, and the San Juan Bautista Mission. At the Carmel Mission there were prints of dog and cat feet in the floor from when the tiles were drying. It was very cute! We even had the privilege of going to Mass at the Mission the following morning. Carmel was a really quaint little town right on the ocean, with over 400 shops, including galleries, restaurants, cafes and boutiques. It was not only a great place to shop, but it also had a wonderful beach that even allowed dogs. We were also fortunate enough to see adorable sea otters in Carmel and had a great time watching their hilarious antics through our binoculars.

After Carmel, we went to San Francisco to visit Uncle Jack, Aunt Juliana, Dad's cousins Jack and Sally, and Uncle Jack's adorable dog Smokey. After a delicious meal with them we journeyed to the next park, Point Reyes National Seashore. We stayed there for three days before heading off to our next stop, Lassen Volcanic National Park. It was one of our favorite parks, even though Jenna almost broke her finger there. From Lassen, we went to our second to last stop, Lava Beds National Monument. We stayed there for two days of cave-exploring before driving back to Oregon for our last stop, Crater Lake National Park. After visiting this beautiful lake inside a collapsed volcano, we headed down the road for home.

This book is unusual in the sense that it is written by kids for kids. Most guidebooks are written about what adults think is interesting, not what kids like. This book is written from a kid's point of view, and focuses on the aspects of the parks that kids would enjoy. Since we are kids ourselves, we are experts in this field.

At first, writing this book seemed like an impossible task. After all, we are only 12 and 14 years old! But after we started, we realized that all we had to do was take it step by step, park by park. Before we knew it, it was done! We hope that our writing of this book has inspired all the other potential young authors to write their own book. We also hope you enjoy our book and find it helpful as you explore the national parks yourselves.

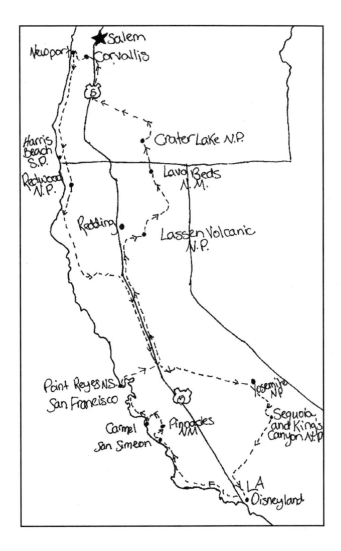

R edwood National Park

"The redwoods, once seen, leave a mark or create a vision that stays with you always...they are not like any trees we know. They are ambassadors from another time."

~John Steinbeck

T he first recorded European sighting of a redwood tree occurred October 10, (which is our Grandmother's birthday!), 1769, when Father Ivan Crespi of the historic Portola Expedition described in his journal "some very high trees." That was the understatement of the century!! He wasn't kidding, they're high! Redwood National Park is home to the tallest trees in the world. The park stretches along the coast from near Crescent City to Orick, and also includes some land that is inland, which borders Redwood Creek.

If you ever meet a redwood tree in your travels, be sure to stand at the base and look up the massive trunk. These trees are so tall they made us feel like Lilliputians from *Gulliver's Travels*. Did you know that some redwood trees are taller than a soccer field is long? The branches of the trees are way up at the top because that is where the sunlight is available for them to photosynthesize. When you are walking in the forest, it is really dark and there aren't very many under-story plants. This is because the branches at the top of the trees prevent much sunlight from reaching the ground. While in the redwoods, we felt very small and insignificant. The branches being hundreds of feet above the ground and the scarcity of undergrowth added to our feeling of smallness.

When most people go to Redwood National Park, they are lazy and just see the major tourist attractions, like the Big Tree. Even though the Big Tree is fun to see, and is 93 m (304 ft) tall, it doesn't give you the feeling of being in an actual redwood forest; besides, a fence surrounds it. So, it is really

These are some of the beautiful, massive redwood trees. You have to go in the forest, away from the crowds to experience a redwood forest.

important to walk on the trails into the redwood forest, even if just for five minutes. The feeling of being in a redwood forest is different from being in any other forest we have ever been in. It is hard to describe exactly why the forest feels different, but we think that it has something to do with the trees being so tall and the branches being so high up.

Redwoods don't grow well right next to the ocean because the air is too salty and it's too windy. Sitka spruces do better under those conditions. Just a short distance from the beach live the redwoods. They get a lot of their moisture during the almost rainless summer months from a thing called fog drip. This is where the water from the heavy fog collects on tree needles and drips to the ground below. We know fog drip first hand from our camping experiences in Oregon, and think it is really strange. Out in the open, it is not raining at all, but when you go under the trees it's just like a rainy day. When you get to higher elevations above the fog zone in the Coast Range Mountains, there aren't any redwoods. This it because there isn't any fog drip and it's too dry for them to grow in the summer, even though an average of 1.5 to 2.4 m (5 to 8 ft) of rain falls every year.

In the early 1960s, only 15% of the redwood trees remained standing. The rest had been cut down for houses and furniture. The government decided to create a park to protect the few remaining trees, and so, in 1968, Congress passed a law to set aside some land as Redwood National Park. Shortly after, they decided to make the park bigger because the Park Service started to get really worried about erosion. It was threatening to kill the redwoods in the park. The erosion upstream from the park was already naturally high because of the geology and the high amounts of rain. Logging was making the problem worse. A big rainstorm could greatly increase the flow of the stream, dump many feet of sediment around the trees, which could kill them, or erode the streambank and make the trees fall down.

The National Park Service is also concerned about erosion because of its effects on fish and insect habitat in the stream beds of the park. The government decided to make into parkland the land upstream from the original park. They also put restrictions on what private landowners, who lived upstream from the park, were allowed to do on their land.

Our first night at the park, we stayed along the banks of the clear, beautiful Smith River in a campsite surrounded on three sides by colossal redwood trees. The campground was called Jedediah Smith State Park Campground. Redwood National Park is weird because it includes three state parks within its boundaries that were there before the national park was formed. Jedediah Smith is the best campground we have ever stayed at. It is great for both RV's and tents, so be sure to get your reservation in early to get a site. We stayed in site number 75, which was right on the Smith River. It was a great site because it was right in the tall trees and we were also next to a roaring river. The Smith River is a big, deep, fast flowing, cold, and really pretty river. It is a beautiful emerald green color with gigantic redwoods on either side. Although the river is freezing cold, the bravest of the brave, like us, jumped in anyway! A huge rock opposite our site offered shelter from the current and provided a deep calm pool, which made perfect conditions for swimming, however briefly. We thought that the current was kind of dangerous when we were there in early June, but the pool behind the rock provided a safe refuge from the swift flowing waters and made for safe swimming. If you want to do some serious swimming, be aware that the Smith River is cold all year-round, but that the park offers some warmer, safer swimming spots in Redwood Creek later on in the summer.

After a couple of nights at Jedediah Smith Campground, we moved to Prairie Creek Campground, which is in Prairie Creek State Park, another of those little parks in the park. It is really pretty, but not quite as pretty as Jedediah Smith. It was a great spot to view the many elk that inhabit the area. We saw over one hundred elk at one time right from our site! The campground is situated at the boundary of a redwood forest and a huge meadow. The forest provided many beautiful hiking trails and huge trees, and the meadow provided the elk. It was really peaceful. The elk were all female, but as we discovered from our expeditions in the area, many bull elk roam here too. The elk graze in that meadow year-round because they like to eat grass, so you have a pretty sure chance of seeing them. Although they are cute and furry animals, beware of their antlers and hooves; they can be dangerous, especially in the fall during breeding season.

This is an elk near the campground in Prairie Creek State Park. We saw hundreds at a time!

Some other interesting animals you might see in this park are black bears and bobcats, both of which are common. You also might see the rare face of a mountain lion, the cute river otters, the stinky skunks, or the sly weasels. Some animals you might see along the coast are harbor seals, elephant seals, sea lions, gray whales, and dolphins.

The nicest hiking trail we found in the park leaves from the road just a short distance north of the Prairie Creek Campground. There is a trailhead on the west side of the road. This trail is a great place to get away from the people and really experience the redwoods. Even if you are pressed for time, we still recommend taking a short hike on this trail. To really enjoy the redwoods, you have to be there alone, and you definitely won't find solitude at the campground.

One of the best things to do while in Redwood National Park is to take a detour to Gold Bluffs Beach and Fern Canyon. Our dad asked us if we wanted to go to a very special place that he had visited 20 years ago. He told us it would be a mystery trip and he wouldn't tell us where we were going. He did tell us it would take a long time to get there, but by then we were so curious that we didn't mind a long car ride. A winding, narrow, dirt road led us to our destination. It was a very long drive, but it was worth it! Along the way, there were lots of opportunities to see bull elk, which are seldom seen in the campgrounds or in the meadow. We saw at least one six-point bull, (a bull that has six points on each of its antlers) while driving. When you get to Gold Bluffs Beach, you'll probably notice that it's a very wild and windy beach with big waves. Although it is too dangerous to swim here, the beach is a wonderful place to camp. At the top of the beach there are cliffs, golden in color, which give the beach its name. While you're there, be sure to look for the bull elk that spend a lot of their time in small groups or alone on the beach.

Farther along the dirt road, you have to drive through a stream. We were afraid that we would get stuck, but while we were trying to decide if we should risk the crossing, Dad stepped on the gas. Luckily we ended up on the other side safely. The road ends in a small parking lot, where the trailhead to Fern Canyon is located. If you have ever seen the movie *Fern Gully*, the canyon in the movie looks just like Fern Canyon. This canyon's beauty made it one of our favorite stops on the whole trip. The stream blocks the entrance to the trail. Mom wanted to turn back, but we convinced her to keep going and found ourselves in one of the most beautiful places we had ever seen. It was late afternoon and there were no other people there, so we had the whole place to ourselves. The walls of the canyon were lined with lush, green ferns, and they dripped with tiny waterfalls that splashed on our heads as they fell to the pebbles.

Fern Canyon is only for the adventurous. We ended up having to cross that stream on logs about 30 times, and on one crossing Jenna accidentally stepped into the stream and soaked her shoe, so if you go you might want to bring an extra pair of socks and dry shoes. If you do accidentally fall into the stream, you'll probably dry quickly as Jenna did in the warm air.

Being in Fern Canyon was like being in a fairy tale. It was so magical that we expected fairies and sprites to pop out from behind fern fronds any moment. We took lots of pictures, but none of them captured the canyon's beauty. The many bright shades of green and the sound of the running brook and the tiny waterfalls cascading down the fern-covered walls made the canyon impossible to capture in a regular "Kodak moment."

We were very apprehensive about including Fern Canyon in our book because it was so special and we didn't want it to become overcrowded. But the National Park Service offers lots of information about it and so we changed our minds and decided to put it in. This was the only place we hesitated to discuss in the book. Our dad had been there 20 years ago and the canyon was still in the same perfect condition as he had seen it then. Please treat this special place with extra care so you and your children might be able to enjoy it in the years to come as much as we did. As for us, we plan a return trip as soon as possible. Maybe we'll see you there!

One afternoon, we decided to drive up Bald Hills Road and check out the Bald Hills Prairie. We wanted to see it because Leonel Arguello, the scientist we interviewed, said that it was his favorite place in the park. The prairie is a pretty grassland with scattered oak trees and flowers. It was fun to see, but it wasn't one of our favorite places in Redwood National Park. We are pretty sure that the reason Mr. Arguello liked it so much is because he is a botanist and Bald Hills probably has more plant species than anywhere else in the park. So, if you are into botany, you should definitely go on a hike here.

Interview

Name: Leonel Arguello
Position in the Park: Botanist

Q. *Where is your favorite place to go in Redwood National Park?*
A. For a day trip, Bald Hills is my favorite and for overnight Jedediah Smith.

Q. *Where is your favorite campground?*
A. Jedediah Smith State Park Campground by the Smith River.

Q. *What are your favorite things to do while in the park?*
A. The best things to do are beach combing and bird watching.

Q. *Where is your favorite place to hike?*
A. Bald Hills is the best. There are no trails; you can just walk through the prairie.

Picture of Bald Hills Prairie in Redwood National Park. We had fun driving and walking around up there.

Q. When is the best time to come to the park?

A. The best time to come is from July to the rainy season (mid fall).

Q. Are there any good places to swim?

A. The Smith River is cold all the time. Redwood Creek and Klamath are good places, if you can find a swimming hole.

Q. Are there any good bike trails?

A. That's one thing the park needs—some more bike trails. Prairie Creek State Park has some, but they are difficult trails for racing bikers. The people who are really in shape go on those trails.

Yosemite National Park

"At present the valley is like a grand hall, its walls covered with fine paintings and perfect in every way, and the floor covered with a beautiful carpet, but torn and dusty in some spots..."
~ *John Muir, June 21st, 1889*

We have been to tons of national parks and Yosemite is one of our favorites, despite the crowds. It is hard to tell exactly what makes Yosemite so special, but we think that it has to do with the huge, beautiful waterfalls and the spectacular sheer vertical cliffs. No wonder artists and photographers flock here; the scenery is more impressive than anywhere we have ever been.

Yosemite Valley is the center of all activities in Yosemite National Park. The scenery is most spectacular in and around the valley, most of the people are there and there are lots of things to do. Although there are many other really cool places in the park, most people end up in the valley. We feel that a trip to Yosemite wouldn't be complete without visiting the valley. The only problem with Yosemite's grandeur is that it brings millions of people each year. This sometimes causes overcrowding in the valley, especially during the summer months. Fortunately, the Park Service recognizes this problem, and has decided to make a Yosemite Valley Plan. This plan is designed to minimize the effects of people on the valley, in an attempt to make it as natural as possible. One of the main things they are focusing on is to get fewer cars in the valley, because cars cause air pollution and congestion and that's not what a national park is supposed to be all about.

The Merced River flows through Yosemite Valley. The valley is unique for several different reasons. It was carved by the river and then was carved deeper by glaciers at least three separate times during the last ice age. The ice was so high, only the tallest things, such as El Capitan and Half Dome, poked above the top. The ice was so thick that the weight of it carved the valley very deep. This is the whole reason that there are high waterfalls. Upper Yosemite Falls is the second highest free-leaping waterfall in the world, and it cascades an amazing 435 m (1,427 ft). The combined Upper, Middle, and Lower Yosemite Falls drop a total of 740 m (2,428 ft) making it one of the highest waterfalls in the world. There was a massive piece of ice in the valley that carved the valley floor down. The smaller tributary valleys and streams didn't have as much ice in them, and so they didn't get carved out as much. So the tributaries flow into the valley way up on the canyon walls. These tributaries form Yosemite's beautiful and world-famous waterfalls. As reminders of the earlier ice age, there are still small glaciers! The reason that the valley floor is so flat is because when the ice was melting it left lots of debris, which formed a dam on the Merced River and created ancient Lake Yosemite. The lake was 600 m (2,000 ft) deep! The sediment that washed down the river filled in most of the lake with sand and gravel and made the bottom flat. Now, the present level of the valley is a couple thousand feet higher than it used to be.

While in Yosemite Valley, there are many things you shouldn't miss. These include El Capitan, Vernal Falls, Yosemite Falls, Half Dome, and Nevada Falls.

One of our favorite activities while in Yosemite was hiking up to Vernal Falls. You can see it from the valley floor, but it is way more spectacular up close. There is a really pretty trail that goes along the edge of the river right up to the falls. Before you get to the really steep, slippery part, there is a huge rock for those who need a rest. It's a wonderful place to have a picnic and has a really nice view of the falls, but beware of the overly friendly ground squirrels. They have a tendency to not wait to be invited to share your lunch. ☺ Don't feed them, though, because human food is not really good for wildlife. There is also an outhouse and a drinking fountain for those who need them.

For you adventuring types, you can continue on to the top of the falls. This is highly recommended and changes your whole experience of the hike. If your parents don't feel the need to hike up, you can always leave them behind on the picnic rock where they can watch you climb. Young children should not go by themselves, though, because it has a slippery, steep, rock staircase with a sheer 96 m (317 ft) drop-off to a raging river below.

Clark's Nutcracker

Here is a picture of Vernal Falls. On the right side of the falls you can see the mist that we had to walk through to get to the top.

Here is an except from Jenna's journal.

June 5ᵗʰ

We soon came to some rock steps that led up the side of the waterfall. As we went up, I saw a bunch of wet hikers coming down and above me I could see a wall of mist, so my hopes were totally aroused and I couldn't wait to break the mist wall. Also, from there, I had a spectacular view of Vernal Falls. As we ascended the steps, we began to get misted. The steps got wet and kind of slippery, so Mom made us stay right next to her. As we got higher, the view got even more spectacular, and we got wetter. Soon we were right next to the waterfall, and the view was breathtaking. There was even a little rainbow caused by the mist. That view was right up there with Fern Canyon as one of the most beautiful places I have ever seen.

~Jenna

Us enjoying the beauty of Mirror Lake. On a calm day, you can't tell the reflection from the real thing!

Another hike we took was to Mirror Lake. We must confess that we were very disappointed after Vernal Falls. We liked the fact that it was handicapped-accessible, but the trail in was like a 4-lane highway. Mirror Lake itself is rather small and it reminded us of a little mud-hole. It is one of the most popular tourist-attractions in the park, so it was very crowded. Even though the hike isn't the best, the real plus is the view from the shore. Directly in front of you is Half Dome, and it reflects beautifully on the surface of the water. For photographers and artists, this spot can't be beat. It provides some of the prettiest pictures imaginable.

When we first arrived in Yosemite, our parents had to do some work in the library so we got to explore the village. Yosemite Village is unusual in the fact that it is an actual village inside a national park. It has all the features of a village: a post office, grocery store, ice-cream shop, restaurants, art store, and even people living there and attending school!

We had a nice time looking at the many exhibits and interesting buildings in Yosemite Village. We spent some time looking at the museum and learned a lot about the history of the area. The museum's exhibits change regularly, so we can't guarantee what will be there. While we were there, though, we saw a wonderful Native American exhibit and a painting gallery. One thing we can guarantee that will be in the museum is the gift shop. It is a small shop with various knick-knacks and jewelry.

In order to learn more about the area, we also went to the visitor center and a Native American village reproduction located behind the museum. The visitor center gave good insight into how the valley was formed, and did it in a way everyone could understand. There is also a gift shop there, which offered excellent books, maps, postcards, and souvenirs. If you're looking for something to take home with you, this is the place we recommend most.

This is our family on our hike to Vernal Falls. We had a wonderful time hiking up there, and even had fun getting soaked by the mist!

The Native American village was a self-guided tour explaining what is was like to be a Native American in Yosemite a long time ago. There are teepees and other American Indian dwellings that you can walk in and around at your own pace. If you are interested in this kind of thing, this is a great place to go. If not, you should probably skip it.

For all those artists out there, Yosemite Village offers a wonderful opportunity to paint in various media with visiting expert artists. You can sign up for any number of art classes, including watercolor, colored-pencil, acrylic, and more, depending on what they are offering at the time. The classes vary according to when you are there. There is also a store that offers art supplies to those who forgot theirs.

There is always something going on in the village, and one thing we happened to go to while we were there was a theatrical performance about John Muir. An actor named Lee Stetson, who looks remarkably like John Muir's pictures, portrayed the wandering naturalist perfectly in a production called *Conversation with a Tramp, an Evening with John Muir*. Not only was it fun to see, it was also very informative and we learned a lot about the life of an American legend. Mr. Stetson took us back to the time when the beautiful valley of Hetch Hetchy was being flooded to provide drinking water for San Francisco. Hetch Hetchy looked so much like a small version of Yosemite Valley it was nicknamed "Little Yosemite". John Muir fought for years to save this beautiful valley, but, because the government was very shortsighted in this issue, it was flooded anyway. This was said to cause the death of John Muir because he was so disappointed. ☹ To find out more about the life of John Muir, you can look at the report done by Jenna at the end of this chapter.

(Continued on page 35)

Interview

Name: Lee Stetson
Position: Actor in John Muir productions

Q. What role did Muir play in the initiation of the Park Service?

A. He played virtually no part in the actual creation of the Park Service. He died before it was formed. He knew we needed a Park Service, so he advocated for it. In the early days when he was alive, the only people who took care of the parks in an official sense were the U.S. Cavalry and Army. He did play a major role in the creation of Yosemite, though.

Q. How did John Muir directly affect your life?

A. In many, many ways. I first came across the character of John Muir in 1981 when my friend sent me his biography. I didn't know much about the life of John Muir before that. I had hiked in the Sierras though. I thought he was very interesting, so I did some research on his life and the friends around him with the idea of doing a dramatic show. When I discovered more and more of his contributions and astonishing adventures, I was immediately impressed. I asked to try the show out for a few weeks, and now, 18 years later, I have four different productions. I get to travel all over the world, from Scotland to Japan, mainly places Muir had been to himself. It's great fun!

(Continued on page 34)

(Continued from page 33)

Q. *What kind of person do you think John was?*

A. Muir was a very bright, intelligent, articulate, and kind
    gentleman who didn't have the wool pulled over his eyes.
    He could have chosen many different life careers, for he
    was a talented inventor and a solid writer. He decided to
    choose a combination of all his talents. He studied glacial
    action, the big trees of California, geology, and botany as
    well as many other things. He was a great father and a
    good husband.

Q. *Why are the National Parks important? Why did Muir think*
    they were?

A. They are important for so many reasons today, but they
    were just as important in Muir's day. They are a safety
    valve for people who need the help and healing that
    comes from engaging in the wilderness. They are places
    for members of the animal kingdom to live out their
    destiny, and evolve the way they should without man's
    intervention. They are a place of refuge and protection for
    all creation, a place for the peace of mind and relaxation
    of people who need to escape the cities. They are
    laboratories of how the world should really work without
    human impact.

(Continued from page 32)

A great place to go to see giant sequoia trees (if you aren't going to go to Sequoia National Park) is Mariposa Grove. You can either walk the trails by yourself or take a narrated open-air tram ride through the trees. A concessionaire runs the tram and takes you winding through the sequoia grove to see the biggest tree there, the Grizzly Giant. It is 9.5 m (31 ft) in diameter at the base and is believed to be 2,700 years old. They run tram rides about every 2 hours, so if you want to get off and look at something you can just catch the next tram. The tram ride saves a lot of time and energy, but the narration was a bit hokey for us. It does give you a great opportunity to see the gigantic trees up-close, though, and shows you about as much as a hike would.

A fantastic drive from Yosemite Valley leads you to two of the best views in the world. Washburn and Glacier Points allow you to see Half Dome, Nevada and Vernal Falls, Yosemite Village, Liberty Cap, Mirror Lake, and a lot more from 975 m (3,200 ft) above the valley floor. At Glacier Point, you can see spectacular Upper and Lower Yosemite Falls, whereas you can't see it from Washburn. Washburn does offer an amazing profile of Half Dome, though. Glacier Point is famous for its view, so therefore it gets more tourists. Laura personally liked Washburn better, but the whole rest of the family liked Glacier Point better. Regardless of which you prefer, you should definitely see them both. If you do like Washburn better, please write Laura at P.O. Box 609, Corvallis, OR, 97339. ☺

In the old days, people used to drop burning embers off the top of Glacier Point in the evenings to provide entertainment for the people camping in Curry Village below. It was continued as a popular spectacle for many years, and our grandmother got to see it in the 1920s when she traveled there with her brother and his friend in their old-fashioned car. (Grammie was in the rumble seat. She rode all the way from Vancouver, Canada to Mexico in what was basically the trunk of the car. When she got back, she was so sunburned her face was "like shoe-leather." ☹) We are glad that they discontinued this form of entertainment because it wasn't very much in keeping with a national park, but we are sure that it was really fun to see.

(Continued on page 39)

June 7th
    As I was taking in all the beautiful scenery 3,000 ft. below me, a raven came circling up and hovered right at our level, and then circled higher, as if mocking us, that with all of our achievements, we couldn't even go as high as a silly old raven. It would be nice to be a bird, wouldn't it?

                              ~Jenna

A breathtaking view of Yosemite Valley and Yosemite Falls from Glacier Point. This lookout is a very popular place, but it's well worth the drive up there and the crowds.

Interview

Name: Dick Ewart
Position in the Park: Park Ranger

Q. *What is your favorite thing to do in the park?*
A. Hike.

Q. *Where is the best place to hike?*
A. The valley. There are little trails that weave in and around
    the valley. You can hike as little or as much as you want.
    Past Mirror Lake, there is Snow Creek trail. It's really quiet
    and there are not many people.

Q. *When is the best time to visit Yosemite?*
A. All of the year is nice. There are different times for different
    interests. April through June is good for seeing the
    waterfalls and raging rivers because all the snow is melting.
    July through September is good for backpacking. October
    though February is great for snowshoeing and skiing. I like
    April and October the best because there aren't as many
    people around.

Q. *Are there any good swimming holes in Yosemite?*
A. There are no warm places to swim. The river is fed by
    melting snow. It is about 60 degrees even in the summer.

(Continued on page 38)

(Continued from page 37)

Q. Do you think it is best to tent camp, stay at hotels, or stay in an RV while at the park?

A. Personally I like tent camping.

Q. Are there any really good bike trails?

A. The Valley has lots of good bike trails. My favorite is Valley Road in the early morning. Bikes aren't allowed on hiking trails.

Q. Are there any especially pretty scenic drives?

A. All the drives here are pretty. The best thing to do is buy Yosemite Road Guide. It is about $3.50. Throughout the park, there are markers with codes on them. This book corresponds with the codes and tells you a little about the place you are at. If my friends are coming up and I don't have enough time to show them around, I send them the book and tell them to take a tour on their own with the book.

Q. What is the major activity that you would recommend to kids visiting the park?

A. Hiking. The most important thing is that people need to get out of their car. Out in the world, you drive here, drive there, and when you come to Yosemite, you drive too. So you need to get our of your car and walk around. It can be a small walk, medium walk, or whatever suits you. Sit on a rock and watch the view and be part of nature.

(Continued from page 36)

For those serious hikers out there, there is a trail from Glacier Point down to Curry Village which should be a spectacular way to see the valley, and get some exercise in the process.

One of the things you might notice from these high vantage points is the many layers of different vegetation. It starts with chaparral in the lowest parts of the park. Chaparral is the shrubby vegetation with hardly any trees because of its dry climate. Then, as you get higher, you get to some oak forests with juniper and pine trees. Next comes the mixed-conifer forest, which features ponderosa pine and several other tree species. You can tell a ponderosa pine tree by its really long needles that come in bunches of threes and its bark that looks like a jigsaw puzzle. Above the mixed-conifer forest comes the fir and lodgepole pine forests. You can tell lodgepole pine trees by their short needles in bunches of twos. Another feature of the lodgepole pines is that they are straight and narrow, perfect for the needs of the Native Americans who used them to hold up their lodges, hence the name "lodgepole". After that is the sub-alpine region, where some of the trees are short and stunted from the heavy wind, and then about 14% of the park is alpine tundra up towards the highest peaks. Up there, there are no trees because the climate is too harsh. A few hardy species of plants brave the weather up there by sticking close to the ground though. Because of all these different kinds of vegetation, there are also many different wildlife species in and around the park.

One of the most enjoyable things to do while in Yosemite Valley is to go around and see all the beautiful sites. There are many different ways you can do this. The park offers free shuttles that can take you around the valley. There are stops in all of the major spots, and you can get on and off when you want. You can also rent bikes in Curry Village or at Yosemite Lodge. There are many paved bike paths that can take you almost anywhere you want to go. You can also travel by car, but there aren't very many parking spaces and it's hard to stop when you see something you want to look at more closely.

The best time to sightsee is in the early morning. This is because it's the least crowded then; there is a greater chance to see wildlife; it's prettiest then; and the lighting is really good for pictures. If you are staying at a campground and the rest of your family is lazy or still sleeping, you can take the shuttle by yourself if you want. You can get all your sightseeing and photography done and be back before they even wake up. Be sure to clear it with your parents first, though!

One of the neatest things to see is the rock climbers on El Capitan. Make sure to bring binoculars, because they look microscopic compared to the size of the rock. There is a meadow near the base of El Capitan along the road where a few rock climbers gather and watch their friends scale the cliff. This is a great place to see the climbers on the rock and be able to talk to some people who have or are going to climb El Capitan.

The Ahwahnee Hotel is one of the great historic lodges of the West. If you are traveling with your parents, chances are that one of them will want to see the Ahwahnee Hotel. It was designed by the same person who designed Timberline Lodge on Mt. Hood in Oregon. Inside, there were tons of Native American art pieces and decorations. Although it was fun to see, we really liked Timberline Lodge and the lodges that we stayed at in Glacier National Park (Many Glacier Lodge, East Glacier Lodge, and McDonald Lodge).

Warning all you RV travelers! While there, we witnessed an RV having to back up a curving, one-way drive, because the vehicle couldn't fit under the overhang in front of the hotel. This caused a great commotion and we recommend that you think twice before driving an RV anywhere near the hotel.

We wanted to drive up to Tuolumne Meadows and see the meadows and the alpine areas. Unfortunately, it was still covered with snow while we were there in June, so we were unable to go. We have heard it's really beautiful there, and there are tons of flowers. There are lots of wonderful hiking trails that start in the meadow. We will have to save that for another trip.

While in Yosemite, we were forced to stay in two different campgrounds and at many different campsites because, by the time we made our reservations, it was almost totally full. Actually, we called and booked sites on the first day that they took reservations for the time that we would be visiting. Be sure to get your reservations in really early so you have a chance to visit this beautiful park.

Even though we met some nice people there, we found the campgrounds over-crowded and the sites were really small. There is nothing that can be done about this because there are about four million visitors per year! If you are seeking more space, Wawona Campground, which is out of the valley, offers more room. We were informed by a park employee that some fun things to do while in Wawona are to hike up Chilnualna Creek, learn some history at Wawona museum, and horseback rides can be found behind the history museum. Besides people, there is an occasional bear visiting the campgrounds. So, be sure to keep your food safe.

Jenna shares some thoughts
about John Muir

"Going to the mountains is going home."

~John Muir

Photo of a painting of John Muir by Herbert A. Collins. It was painted about 1908 and is housed in the Muir Woods National Monument. (Photo courtesy of Sierra Club.)

If you've ever been to a National Park, you'll understand exactly what I mean when I say that they are spectacular, jewels of the USA. They remind us of a time when people didn't make huge buildings. Instead, people lived in closer harmony with nature. For these gorgeous places, we can mainly thank one man: John Muir. This man's life's work has touched all of us in many ways, and I am here to write about it and to explain how great and wonderful a man he really was.

John Muir was born on April 21, 1838 in Dunbar, Scotland. He lived in a small cottage by the stormy North Sea with his brothers, sisters, and parents (Daniel and Ann Gilrye). He attended the local school until he was eleven, and he spent his free-time roaming the beautiful countryside, enjoying nature.

Muir was always a big nature lover. He once said, "None of nature's landscapes are ugly so long as they are wild."

In 1849, when Muir was eleven, his family immigrated to the United States, settling first at Fountain Lake and then moving to Hickory Hill Farm near Portage, Wisconsin.

Muir's father was a hard-working man who believed in work and discipline. He worked his family from dawn to dusk, and John barely had any time to do what he loved: explore the natural world. In his sparse free time, John and his younger brother would roam the fields and forests of the rich Wisconsin countryside. Muir became a very good observer and also an ingenious inventor. He made clocks that kept accurate time and created a wonderful device that tipped him out of bed - before dawn! ☺

In 1860, Muir took his many inventions to the state fair at Madison, where he won many prizes and gained much admiration. Also in 1860, Muir enrolled in the University of Wisconsin. He was 22. He made good grades, but at 25 he left Madison in favor of odd-jobbing his way through the northern United States and Canada.

In 1867, Muir was working at a carriage parts shop in Indianapolis. While he was there, he suffered a blinding eye injury. A month later, when he regained his sight, Muir resolved to turn his precious vision to the fields and forests. That began John Muir's years as a wanderer. He walked a thousand miles from Indianapolis to the Gulf of Mexico. From there, he sailed to Cuba, and later to Panama. Then he crossed the isthmus and sailed up the west coast of the U.S. to land in San Francisco in the year 1868 at the age of thirty. Though he would travel around the world, California became his home.

Muir was captivated by California's Sierra Nevada and especially the Yosemite area. Yosemite's breathtaking beauty was a feast for Muir's eyes after living with city surroundings. It was this magnificence that inspired Muir to dedicate the rest of his life to protecting Yosemite as well as other wild places.

At the time, people were just beginning to recognize the greatness and importance of the wilderness. This also meant that people still had much to learn. The government did not protect the wonderful wild places. John Muir made it his life's work to change that. He once said "Thousands of tired, nerve shaken, over-civilized people are beginning to find out that going to the mountains is going home; wildness is a necessity; and that mountain parks and reservations are useful not only as fountains of timber and irrigated rivers, but as fountains of life."

In 1868, Muir walked across the San Joaquin Valley through waist-high flowers and into the high country for the first time. By 1871 he had found living glaciers in the Sierras, and had visualized his controversial theory of the glaciation of Yosemite Valley. This gave him the recognition he would later use to help preserve the wilderness as National Parks.

Beginning in 1874, Muir started writing a series of articles entitled "Studies in the Sierra". That launched his successful career as a writer. He left his beloved mountains and lived for a while in Oakland, California. In 1880, he married Louise Wanda Strentzel, and moved to Martinez, California. There, they raised their two daughters, Wanda and Helen. Muir also went into partnership with his father-in-law and began work at the family fruit ranch. Still the wanderer, Muir's travels took him to Alaska many times, to Australia, South America, Africa, Europe, China, Japan, and of course, again and again to the Sierra Nevada.

He then turned more seriously to writing, publishing 300 articles and 10 major books that recounted his travels. In them he beckoned everyone to "Climb the mountains and get their good tidings." His readers loved the spiritual quality Muir put into his writing out of his love for the high country, and many were inspired and often moved to action by the enthusiasm of Muir's works. Through a series of articles in the *Century* magazine, he drew attention to the devastation of mountain meadows and forests by sheep. He worked to remedy this destruction himself along with *Century's* associate editor, Underwood Johnson. In 1890, due largely to Muir's and Johnson's efforts, Yosemite National Park was created. This was a big triumph for Muir, and he went on to be involved in the creation of Sequoia, Mount Rainier, Petrified Forest, and Grand Canyon National Parks. For all his contributions to the national parks, Muir is often deservedly called the "Father of Our National Park System."

When Johnson and others suggested to Muir that an association should be formed to protect the new Yosemite National Park from the people who were fighting to diminish its boundaries, John formed the Sierra Club in 1892 as a way to "do something for wildness and make the mountains glad." Muir and a number of his determined followers hoped that together they could preserve America's vast natural places - not just for themselves but also for future generations. The Sierra Club gave them a chance to "explore, enjoy, and protect" the earth and translate their concern into action. Muir served as the club's president until his death in 1914.

Muir published *Our National Parks*, a book that caught the attention of President Theodore Roosevelt. In 1903, Roosevelt journeyed to Yosemite to visit Muir, and together they thought up Roosevelt's notable conservation programs. The two of them remained lifelong friends.

Muir and the Sierra Club fought many battles to protect Yosemite and the Sierra Nevada. Probably the most famous and dramatic was the campaign to prevent people from damming the Hetch Hetchy Valley in Yosemite National Park. Muir fought this battle with his heart and soul. He claimed, "Dam Hetch

Hetchy? As well, dam for drinking water the people's churches and cathedrals, for no holier temple was ever consecrated by the heart of man."

Unfortunately, the cause was lost in 1913. The beautiful valley, remarkably like Yosemite, was flooded to become a reservoir for supplying the water needs of the city of San Francisco. The following year, John Muir died of an illness. Some people say that the trauma of losing Hetch Hetchy was the thing that finally did him in.

Whatever the cause of his death, John Muir's works continue to affect us today in the 21st century. The Sierra Club that Muir founded 108 years ago still functions as our protector of the environment. It has grown to 540,000 members, and it has hundreds of committees that strive to save threatened and endangered national resources, scenic areas, and wildlife.

We will always remember John Muir as perhaps the most famous and important naturalist and conservationist in the country. His works affect us greatly more than 100 years later. That wonderful human being was, and still is, a very important voice for the environment through his writing and the Sierra Club. He lived the simple life, and he loved solitary hikes through nature. Muir's unique personality proved just what we needed to protect our fabulous wilderness. He left his imprint on our country in a way that never had been done before. John Muir was a great addition to our list of heroes, and he will always be remembered as one of the best. ☺

Sequoia and Kings Canyon National Parks

"Climb the mountains and get their good tidings. Nature's peace will flow into you as sunshine flows into trees. The winds will blow their own freshness into you, and the storms their energy, while cares will drop off like autumn leaves."

~John Muir

Sequoia and Kings Canyon National Parks are side-by-side so they are easy to visit together. We camped in Sequoia, but got to see some of Kings Canyon too. The difference between the parks is that Sequoia has more different kinds of things to do and Kings Canyon has lots of hiking trails, alpine lakes and wilderness. So if you like the wilderness and backpacking, Kings Canyon is hard to beat. If you go to Kings Canyon National Park, be sure to see the canyon that the park is named after. It happens to be the deepest canyon in the whole country. Also be sure to see the

When you visit Sequoia, you can't help but look up these massive trunks. We certainly couldn't anyway!

largest grove of sequoias in the world at Grant Grove, and the many marble caves. There are at least 180 known caves in these two parks, including one that's 23 km (14 mi) long, the longest cave west of the continental divide. Many rare invertebrates inhabit the caves and some live nowhere else in the world.

June 9th
Today was our first day in Sequoia. We did nothing but photocopy for Dad. It was awful. By the end of the day my head hurt and I didn't feel very good. I soon got over it, but all I have to look forward to is another day of copying. Yuck!

~Jenna

June 10th
Work again today. I ran out of paper, so I had to go back to Dad's building to get more. When I reached down for the paper on the floor, a scorpion stung my hand. It really hurt, but the stinging went away after a few minutes and I'm back to copying again. But what a surprise! I've never seen a scorpion (that wasn't in a zoo) before.

~Laura

After two days of photocopying at Park Headquarters, we finally got to have some fun. There are lots of really interesting and fun things to do while in both Sequoia and Kings Canyon National Parks.

We hiked up a beautiful trail to Tokopah Falls in Sequoia National Park. We saw lots of wildflowers, including monkey flower and a pretty pink flower that we'd never seen before called Indian pink. We also saw a marmot, lots of birds, and a blue butterfly. If you ever hear a high-pitched loud whistle in the mountains, it's probably a marmot. We successfully taught ourselves how to imitate their distress-call, and succeeded in alarming two marmots and causing them to run right by us and dive into their holes. Jenna is really good at imitating them. She

and the marmots carry on regular conversations. ☺ A hummingbird swooped really close to us on the way back. It was really cool. The Tokopah Falls trailhead is located right in the Lodgepole Campground, and the hike is great and leads up to a pretty stair-step waterfall. If you want a really long hike, you can take the trail to Aster Lake from the Wolverton trailhead. It's a great hike to see the sub-alpine and alpine lakes in the Sequoia high country. It is a pretty long hike, though, so you might consider taking camping gear to spend the night.

Marmots are abundant in Sequoia and Kings Canyon National Park. Jenna had fun imitating their distress calls, and found it amusing when they all answered back.

The highlight of Sequoia National Park is, obviously, its sequoia trees. A great place to see these magnificent trees is Giant Forest. We went there and had an enjoyable experience viewing the majesty of the huge trees. Sequoias are not as tall as redwoods, but they are much bigger around and live to be much older. Whereas redwoods live to be between 1,000 and 2,000 years old, sequoias live about 3,000 years. The oldest trees in the world, the bristle cone pine, peak the charts at 4,000 years. They can be found just east of this park, but aren't as magnificent because they aren't very big.

The biggest tree in the world, the General Sherman tree, lives in Giant Forest. We found it very interesting to see, but advise you not to just stop and see it but to look at all the other huge trees as well. Even though they might be a tiny bit smaller than the General Sherman, they are just as spectacular and shouldn't be ignored. It's hard to understand how big these trees really are, but we figured out that if we held hands with 18 of our cousins, we could just barely reach all the way around one of the big ones. We had a really nice time running around and through the House and Senate trees. They were the prettiest groups of sequoia trees we've ever seen. Although most books say that the General Sherman tree is the biggest living thing in the world, they are actually wrong. If you can believe it, there is a mat of fungi under the forest floor in the Pacific Northwest old-growth forests that is really bigger than the tree. It can stretch over miles!

Here we are looking up a giant sequoia trunk.

If you see a forest fire in Sequoia National Park - or any other park for that matter - don't panic (although you should definitely report it to the Park Service). This fire might be a planned fire started by the Park Service in order to reduce fast-burning undergrowth to prevent a huge fire in the future that may destroy all of the forest. These man-made fires actually help the beautiful giant sequoia trees survive, because their seedlings need fire to regenerate.

Most forest fires that aren't man-made are in the middle elevations. This is because the highest forests don't have as much fuel and are usually too wet to burn very far even though the lightning which causes fires strikes there the most; the lowest elevation areas are too low for very much lightning to strike. This also is why fire-loving trees like the sequoia grow in these middle elevations. Since the late 1800s, people thought natural forest fires were a very bad occurrence, and fought to put them out. In doing this, they actually caused, in some cases, huge fires that were impossible to douse that did a lot of damage to many of our forests. This also made some of our forests unhealthy, because tree species like the sequoia, ponderosa pine, and many others need fire to survive. A classic and well-known example of this human error was the huge fire in Yellowstone in the 1980s that destroyed a lot of the trees. We visited this beautiful park a few years ago, and there was still major damage left over from that fire. Now that the Park Service knows the problem, they are fighting to keep fires a regular occurrence in the parks. This isn't easy, because when people go there they don't want to have it all smoky from a fire. We both disagree, though, because we feel that it's more important to preserve the health of these wonderful forests than it is to have a smoke-free visit.

If you're interested in caves, there is a huge cave under Giant Forest called Crystal Cave that offers tours. It has about 10,000 feet of passageways, and it is limestone that has metamorphosed under heat and pressure to form marble. It has all the nice cave features: stalactites, stalagmites, etc. There are lots of good caves (but no tours) in Kings Canyon National Park, but we unfortunately didn't get to visit them. There is also a cave just outside Kings Canyon National Park, called Boyden Cave, that is open to the public for guided tours.

Dogwoods are mixed in with the huge giant sequoia trees.
Jenna and Dad made us stop the car in order to take their
pictures. Aren't they pretty?

Other really cool places to visit that are near Giant Forest are Crescent Meadow and Tharp's Log. Laura wanted to re-name the meadow Crescent Bog, because it was really swampy and there were lots of mosquitoes and other bugs. Don't let the bugs bug you, because Tharp's Log is well worth a couple of bites. You have to take the trail along the edge of Crescent Meadow to get there. Tharp's Log is an old, hollowed-out log that a white settler named Hale Tharp used as a home in the 1800s. It was really neat. He had a bed and a table and a fireplace all inside a huge sequoia tree that had toppled over. There was a window cut into the side and a stone chimney going out the top. Next to it, he had a corral for his animals, and it was right overlooking Crescent Meadow. It was fun to visit because it gave us an insight into what life was like over 100 years ago.

As a finale to our stay in Sequoia, we decided to hike to the top of Morro Rock on the morning before we left the park. Morro Rock is a huge, 91 m (300 ft) tall rock with 400 stone

Mom, Jenna, and Laura enjoying the beautiful view from the top of Morro Rock in Sequoia National Park. We could pick out individual sequoia trees from the others because they are a lot taller than the other trees in the forest.

steps that lead to the top, where you have a breathtaking view of the park and the valley below. It's really neat because you can see how tall the sequoia trees really are, because their tops stick out above the other trees. It wasn't as pretty as Glacier Point in Yosemite, but it still was very beautiful. Take it slow on the way up, because the climb is kind of difficult. If you do get tired, there are benches along the way for rest stops. Keep your eyes peeled for the lizards that inhabit the rock. An un-observant person could miss them totally. From the top of Morro Rock you look down on the San Joaquin Valley. Unfortunately, air pollution gets caught in the valley, especially during the summer, and travels up into the park in the afternoons on the breeze. It causes many problems, including poor visibility, damage to a lot of the trees (especially the yellow pines), and worry that the acid rain from the air pollution may cause the lakes in the park to become overly acidic. This would damage plants and animals that live in the lakes and streams. There are hundreds of small lakes in the high country that are really dilute and similar to the purity of distilled water. (This doesn't mean that you can drink the water without purifying it first. It can still have bugs in it that can make you sick.). This makes them especially sensitive to acid rain because there isn't much in the water to buffer the acidity. Scientists are more worried about air pollution in Sequoia than almost any other national park in the West. So, if you are on top of Morro Rock and can't see much, blame it on the air pollution.

If you are lucky, you might see a bear like we did. We saw a really cute black bear waddling across a log on the forest floor. Even though these bears are cute and furry, you have to remember that they can be very dangerous, especially when protecting their young. So, stay clear of any bear you see, but be sure to notice them because they are a real treat to get to observe. There used to be grizzly bears in the park, but sadly they all got shot. The last known sighting of a grizzly in the park was in 1924. ☹

Black bears live in most of the parks that we visited, but we only saw one in Sequoia.

A really neat thing about Sequoia National Park is its difference in elevation levels. Park headquarters is located at 518 m (1,700 ft), and the tallest peak, Mt. Whitney, reaches 4,418 m (14,494 ft). This is the tallest mountain in the continental United States. This amazing range in elevation causes much variation in temperature and precipitation, and much plant and animal diversity. From the crest of the Sierra Nevada to Death Valley (just outside the park) is almost a sheer drop off! It's a very short distance from the highest point to the lowest point in the country (excluding Alaska)! The drop-off formed when underneath pressure pushed one block of rock up and one down.

Because of so many different plant communities within Sequoia and Kings Canyon National Parks, there are many different species of wildlife. There are even four different species of chipmunks that live at different elevations. Don't confuse the chipmunks with the golden mantle ground squirrels you see in the campground. You can easily tell them apart. Golden mantle ground squirrels are a little bit bigger and they don't have stripes on their head. Chipmunks do. Some other small animals that you can see while hiking in the meadows and in rocky areas are pikas (which are close relatives of the rabbit, and are very small) and marmots. Other animals that are fairly common are coyotes and black bears. If you are really lucky you might be able to see a big horn sheep, wolverine, mountain lion, or bobcat.

Since the air pollution problems in the park have very little to do with campfires, and very much to do with the valley below the park, go ahead and enjoy one of the best places to have a campfire in the West. We stayed at site #163 in Lodgepole Campground, and enjoyed it a lot. If you really want to get into the experience, you can get a campfire song book in Lodgepole Village, including all the words to the old favorites.

Out of all the national parks we visited, Sequoia was located the furthest south. So, it wasn't very hard to drive a little farther south to visit an entirely different kind of park than we had been going to on our adventure. Right after our hike to the top of Morro Rock, we set out on the road to Disneyland. Along the way we stopped at a fruit stand and got oranges, cherries, plums, apricots, cantaloupe, nectarines, strawberries, dates and cashews! This was a big treat for us, because in Oregon fruits and berries were not yet ripe and such variety and freshness were not available in the grocery stores at home. It was a delicious delight.

We spent two jammed-packed, fun-filled days exploring every nook and cranny in Disneyland. We rode all the rides, saw all the sights, and ate all the treats. Our favorite rides were Splash Mountain and Indiana Jones. We talked Mom and Dad into joining us on a couple of rides on Splash Mountain. Mom was a great sport and we brought back a picture of the four of us; we all have our hands up in the air while going off the cliff and Mom is the one with the terrified look on her face! We also really enjoyed the roller coasters. One of the most spectacular things you can do while visiting Disneyland is to go to one of their light shows and night parades. Disneyland's true magical self shines after dark.

Pika

Interview

Name: Annie Esperanza
Position in the Park: Air resources specialist

Q. *What is your favorite thing to do while in Sequoia?*
A. Hiking is the main attraction in the park.

Q. *Where are the best places to hike?*
A. It depends on how much time and energy you have. For a
    short hike, Tharp's Log is nice. It is a huge hollow sequoia
    that Hale Tharp lived in. You can see his log and corral for
    his animals. Tharp wrote that you could see "several bear
    and occasionally a grizzly" in the meadow at one time.
    (We talked to Ms. Esperanza's colleague, Kitty Borden, who
    also told us about Tharp's Log and thought it was a really
    neat place to go). If you climb up Morro Rock, you get a
    great view of the divide and Sequoia Park. It is a 1/4 mile
    climb. The Tokopah Falls Trail is great for scenery, and the
    Congress Trail is a must see.

For longer hikes, the high country near Emerald Lake is
good. It is fun to go up Mt. Whitney, too (you go up Rock
Creek to the Pacific Crest Trail, and then on the John Muir
Trail up the west side of Mt. Whitney). In Kings Canyon,
there are great hikes too, especially in upper Kings Canyon.
I think that Kings Canyon is a little Yosemite with no
people. You can also start at Cedar Grove and do the Rae
Lakes Loop. Cedar Loop is long but is great hiking.
Cottonwood Pass lets you hike at 11,000 to 12,000 feet
(you drive to 10,000 feet in your car to the trailhead), and
it's really fun. Mineral King has tons of great hikes. You
should get a map from the Visitor Center.

Q. *Where are the best campgrounds?*

A. Lodgepole is the best campground because it's in the middle of things. Cedar is good for camping too.

Q. *Which is the best visitors center?*

A. Lodgepole.

Q. *Where are the best scenic drives?*

A. Mineral King is gorgeous and amazing, but remember no RV's are allowed. Crescent Meadow is nice, and the road is good with beautiful trees and those trees you can drive through and on top of.

Q. *When is the best time to go to the park?*

A. If you want to ski, February and March are good because the days start to get longer and the snow is good. For hiking, it's best to go in August or September, but all the trails usually open in June.

Q. *Are there any good places to bike?*

A. You can only bike on paved roads and in campgrounds.

Q. *What other interesting information can you tell us about the park?*

A. There were several proposed developments for this park, which luckily did not happen. Disney wanted to build a ski resort in Mineral King, but environmental groups led by the Sierra Club stopped them.

Note: Ms. Esperanza told us she used to be a backcountry ranger on horseback in Lassen Volcanic National Park. We both think this would be a really cool job! ☺

Some very interesting snow plants. Everyone found them photogenic- a professional photographer was taking pictures of them! They are totally red. They don't have any green leaves because they don't photosynthesize, but live instead on decaying vegetation.

Plate 1. While hiking in the gorgeous Fern Canyon in Redwood
National Park, we had to cross this small stream many
times. We crossed on logs every time, and once Jenna
accidentally stepped in! She had to proceed with one wet
shoe and one dry shoe, but that didn't spoil the fun.

Plate 2. The spectacular Yosemite Falls; our favorite waterfall in
Yosemite National Park.

Plate 3. From the inside of Fern Cave in Lava Beds National Monument, we marveled at all the lush ferns growing at the entrance. You can see the ladder we climbed down on; it really is a magical place!

Plate 4. View of Crater Lake from Crater Lake Lodge. This is one of the most beautiful lakes we have ever seen. Crater Lake National Park.

Pinnacles National Monument

"I should be telling this with a sigh,
Somewhere ages and ages hence,
Two roads diverged in a yellow
wood,
And I,
I took the one less traveled by,
And that has made all the
difference."
~Robert Frost

At first, neither of us liked Pinnacles National Monument at all. We found it very uninteresting and we couldn't imagine what there would be that would be fun to do there. It was extremely hot, and the only relief we got was taking a swim in the pool at the campground that is just outside the park. We couldn't understand what was so special about the park. There were no spectacular waterfalls, huge trees, or beautiful rivers. We just didn't get it. The next day though, we took a hike up to a talus cave called Balconies Cave, and we then came to appreciate the real beauty of the park.

The main attraction of Pinnacles National Monument is definitely hiking. If you aren't into hiking, this might not be the place for you, but bird watching, rock climbing, and wildflowers are also very popular. The hikes there are very beautiful, but you should consider going early to beat the heat of the middle of the day. In the summer, Pinnacles is certainly a hot place, but don't let the heat keep you from having fun outside. We recommend a visit during spring or fall to avoid the summer heat.

A nice hike we recommend is the one we took, the hike along Chalone Creek up to Balconies Cave. It is a beautiful hike that takes you all the way across the whole monument, through interesting caves and past lots of scenic vegetation. The hike takes you right up to some cool rock formations called the pinnacles (the reason for and the name-sake of the monument). They are the eroded remains of an ancient volcano, which erupted many millions of years ago. They are very interesting to see, and the monument was established by President Theodore

Pinnacles National Monument was set aside to preserve the pinnacles rock formation and the talus caves that formed when giant rocks broke off and tumbled down to the bottom of the valley.

Rock climbers enjoy the pinnacles but have to be careful not to disturb any raptors. (Photo courtesy of National Park Service)

Roosevelt to protect them for future generations to enjoy. Pretty much the whole monument used to be a couple hundred miles south, but the land has been gradually moving north along the San Andreas Fault, which is located about 6 km (4 mi) east of the monument.

Balconies Cave itself is a great example of a talus cave. It was formed when huge chunks of rock fell down from the pinnacles and cliffs during earthquakes. All the rocks tumbled down to the bottom of the valley and created a huge pile of boulders. The spaces between these boulders made the talus caves. As a result, there are some places in the caves where you can look up through the boulders and see the sky, and other spots where you can't see anything at all. If you do decide to go to these caves, we highly recommend that you bring a flashlight, because it can get very dark in there, and it's a place where it is easy to trip and fall over loose rocks or fall down cliffs. Actually, if you don't have a flashlight, you have a good chance of falling and breaking your neck; so bring one! There are many ten-foot cliffs and steep climbs scattered throughout the caves.

Not only are these caves fun to look at and explore, they are necessary habitats for many animals. They provide roosting sites and maternity habitat for many kinds of bats. Bear Gulch Cave is even home to a colony of Townsend's big-eared bats, a species of special concern. That species' population has been rapidly declining due to human disturbance to their roosting sites and maternity colonies. Now there are only 37 known colonies left in California, and one of those is in Pinnacles. Bear Gulch Cave is closed to the public indefinitely to protect the bats. Balconies Cave is subject to temporary closures. Balconies Cave is about 121 m (400 ft) long, and Upper Bear Gulch Cave is 490 m (1600 ft) long! So, there is lots of room for bats to roost and raise their young.

Pinnacles National Monument is a really dry park. It only rains about 43 cm (17 in) per year and most of that rain falls in the winter half of the year. So, it's almost, but not quite, a desert. Many plants can't survive the dry conditions, but the ones that can survive have interesting adaptations to help them cope with such a difficult environment. Most of the vegetation in Pinnacles doesn't include very many trees because it is so dry. The vegetation type is called chaparral. Some chaparral trees drop their leaves in the summer to prevent water loss during respiration. (They have to open the little pores, called stomata, to respire.) Many of the chaparral shrubs also have very thin needle-like leaves or a waxy coating over the leaves, which also helps the plant minimize water loss. Two important places in California that protect large areas of chaparral are Pinnacles National Monument and the southwestern part of Sequoia National Park. Pinnacles is a very important place because it is about 80% chaparral. Many of the other places that have this kind of vegetation have been turned into cities, places for people's houses, vineyards, and grazing lands. The preservation

One of the picturesque old Spanish missions that we visited on our way to Pinnacles National Monument.

of chaparral vegetation in Pinnacles is going to become more and more important in California as humans continue to build their developments and remove the natural vegetation.

Pinnacles National Monument is home to many different animal species. These include deer, bobcat, fox, coyote, mountain lion, wild pig, snakes, birds, bees, bats, and many more. There are 13 different species of snake, including the Pacific coastal rattlesnake. There is a big problem with the wild pigs there. The European settlers introduced them in the 1700s, and as their population grows, they continue to destroy the vital vegetation along the streams. To solve this problem, the Park Service is building a fence around the entire monument, removing all the pigs from the inside, and keeping the others out.

There are also many birds of prey in the park, such as prairie falcons, red-tailed hawks, barn owls, and lots of others. Many of them nest on the cliffs and pinnacles in the monument, and are necessary to keep a balanced food chain.

The park hired a bee specialist to come out and do research on the local bees. He thought he would be lucky if he found 200 species living there, because chaparral is known to be really good habitat for bees. He was astounded, as was the Park Service, to find 410 species, 13 of which previously had never been discovered. The more time he spent looking, the more species he found! Pinnacles may have more different species of bees than anywhere else in North America!

June 18th

Today we got up really early and took a long hike through the monument. (We literally got 0 .6 miles from the west side of the park, although we started on the east side of the park). The hike up was nice, but very very hot. It felt like a hundred degrees. All the way up, Laura and I talked about what our new house, that we are looking to buy, should be like. We had envisioned a garden with a stream, fountain, and pool in it, with sunflowers, a cutting garden, lettuce, tomatoes, carrots, cantaloupe, chives, onions, squash, peas, beans and strawberries. We also want lots of fruit trees surrounding it. Anyway, we hiked up to a talus cave. By the time we got there, I was hot, tired and thirsty. We brought water, but it was so gross it almost made me throw up! Dad made me drink it anyway because he didn't want me to get dehydrated. I think he wanted to torture me. This cave, though, was pretty cool *(in more ways than one!). I was really thankful to get out of the heat of the day. The cave was really neat. It was pitch black so we had to use a flashlight. When we came out of the other side of the cave, mom took off her fanny-pack so she wouldn't have it in a picture. Then, we went back through the cave and began our trek back to our car. After 45 minutes of walking, Mom exclaimed "My fanny pack! It's gone!" We realized that she had left it on the ground after taking that picture. Dad got kind of huffy and stormed off to get it. We spent about an hour and a half getting bitten by mosquitoes, playing tic-tack-toe in the dirt, playing with ants, and drinking disgusting water. Finally, Dad came back, thankfully carrying the fanny pack, which contained the car keys, Mom's driver's license, about $200, and Mom's camera and sunglasses. Dad had seen a bunch of wild pigs on the way back! We didn't see them; too bad. All was well.*

~Jenna

Interview

Name: Chad Moore
Position in the Monument: Natural resource scientist

Q. *What is your favorite thing to do in the monument?*
A. Hiking.

Q. *What is your favorite place to go hiking in the monument?*
A. I like to hike out on the old pinnacles trail and explore the Balconies Caves and the Balconies Cliff area. Find a little spot by the creek and sit still and let nature come to you.

(Continued on page 68)

(Continued from page 67)

Q. *Are there any good places to swim?*

A. No, there aren't any warm swimming areas.

Q. *Where is your favorite place to camp?*

A. East Pinnacles Campground. There is no camping inside the monument.

Q. *Would you rather go tent camping or camp in an RV?*

A. If you enjoy sleeping in a tent, that's the way to do it.

Q. *Are there any good bike trails?*

A. There are no bike trails in the monument, but there might be in a few years.

Q. *Where is the best scenic drive?*

A. All of highway 25 is scenic. It is a winding road where you can see wildlife such as antelope, eagles, bobcats, and coyotes.

Q. *What is your favorite thing about the park?*

A. It's one of the quietest places that I know of. To really experience it, you have to listen to the sounds of nature.

Q. *What do you need to be careful of while visiting the park?*

A. Poison oak, rattlesnakes, tarantulas, scorpions, and mountain lions. There are no bears here though.

Q. *What is the best time to visit the park?*

A. Temperatures are pleasant in the spring through mid-June. Most visitors come during that time to see the wildflowers. Fall has fewer visitors but the weather is just as nice as spring.

Point Reyes National Seashore

"If there is magic on this planet, it is contained in water...its substance reaches everywhere; it touches the past and prepares the future; it moves under the poles and wanders thinly in the heights of air."

~Loren Eiseley

The reason we liked Point Reyes National Seashore was because of its beautiful coastline, great bird watching, wide-open spaces, and gorgeous, untamed beaches. We think it is really amazing that such a wild place like this is so close and accessible to a big city like San Francisco. The park boasts rolling grassy hills, high cliffs that are battered by ocean waves, a long windswept beach, sheltered coves that are home to many different marine mammals, peaceful estuaries, and a forest-covered ridge.

On our way to Point Reyes we took a side trip to our Uncle Jack and Aunt Juliana's house, near San Francisco. We hadn't seen them in a while and we had a great visit. Between visiting, we swam in their pool, picked some lemons, had a delicious home-cooked father's day meal with them and our dad's cousin Jack and his wife Sally, and took a walk with their dog Smokey. Smokey is the second best dog in the world after our dog Maggie! Actually her name isn't really Maggie, it's Maggalena Haggalena Oopa Walka Dalka Talka Oka Moka Poka Chagagaga Manchagagaga Chubunga Gungama! Since everyone has trouble remembering it, we call her Maggie ☺. She is half lab, half golden retriever. She has a really sweet personality, and to know her is to love her! Anyway, after the nice visit with Uncle Jack, Aunt Juliana, and Smokey, we stopped for a tour of Jack and Sally's new house, which wasn't far from Point Reyes. It was really fun to see Jack and Sally again.

Waves crash into cliffs along the shore in Point Reyes. (Photo courtesy of National Park Service)

Point Reyes National Seashore has many short hikes that start near the Visitors Center. One of our favorites was the Earthquake Trail. It is a paved loop trail that takes you along a section of the San Andreas Fault. It's really neat because it goes right by a fence that was split in two! One half stayed right where it was and the other half moved about 20 ft! This happened during one of the many earthquakes that were centered on this fault. Actually, the earthquake that moved the fence was the 1906 earthquake that did so much damage to San Francisco. It wasn't centered in San Francisco; the earthquake was centered in Olema, right next to Point Reyes! We thought it was really amazing that the ground shifted so much and that the two halves of the fence moved so far apart. Twenty feet is about the same distance as the distance across both of our rooms put together! We both thought that it would be really weird to be standing by the fence when it was torn apart by the force of the earthquake. Along the trail, there are signs that tell you about the geology of the area, earthquakes, and the San Andreas Fault. We recommend this hike, because it is really interesting and it doesn't take a long time.

Another good, short hike to take is the one to the Native American village. To get there, you have to walk through a grove of eucalyptus trees. It smelled really good to Mom and us, but Dad thought it stunk. For kids not from California, hiking in a grove of eucalyptus trees is an experience. The trail is called Kule Loklo. The village is a replica of a Coast Miwok Native American village. It has information signs and dwellings from Coast Miwok culture from over a hundred years ago. We thought it was fun to see what a Coast Miwok village looked like and to imagine what it would be like to live there.

After you come back from the village, you can stop and see the Morgan Horse Ranch. It was built in 1970 to keep the horses of the park rangers. There are still horses there being used by the park rangers for trail patrol in the backcountry. They also breed and train Morgans, the first breed of American horse! They were also used by the Civil War Cavalry. We used to do a lot of riding at the horse center at Oregon State University. Laura rode a Morgan named Billy. He was her favorite horse because he had a very nice personality. It was really hard to ride him, though, because he used to be a carthorse and so his signals were all mixed up. Often, when she was riding him, she would give him a signal to do one thing and he would do something exactly opposite.

One of the most interesting things about Point Reyes National Seashore is its geology. The San Andreas Fault runs right between the Point Reyes peninsula and the mainland of California. There is a giant crack that runs between Tomales Bay

The Park Service raises and trains Morgan horses at Point Reyes National Seashore. (Photo courtesy of National Park Service)

and Bolinas Lagoon; it separates the Point Reyes peninsula from the rest of California. Point Reyes sits on one tectonic plate, and the mainland next to it sits on another. The San Andreas Fault runs diagonally to the coast of the western United States, and Point Reyes is located where the fault meets the coastline. Point Reyes and the tectonic plate it is riding on are on a journey! It started about 300 miles to the south, and has been heading north at an average of two inches a year! But it doesn't move at a constant speed. The two tectonic plates have jagged edges that catch on one another. When pressure builds between the two plates they give way and the western one jolts forward. This causes an earthquake. Sometimes it's a huge jolt, like the one of 1906, and sometimes it's very small. The peninsula is continuing to move and so if you sit on the Point Reyes peninsula and wait long enough, you will go all the way up to the coast of Alaska!

Point Reyes itself is made of granite, which is very resistant to erosion because it is a really hard rock. It's actually the second hardest rock (after diamond). The areas on both sides of the point are made of softer rocks and so they have eroded away over the thousands of years that the waves have been crashing into them. Therefore, the point is left sticking out into the ocean between where the other rocks would have been if they hadn't eroded away.

While we were in the seashore, we went to see Point Reyes. Before we drove out, though, we decided to stop at Tomales Bay for a swim. It was a nice place to swim, but the water was pretty cold. Then, we continued out to the point. As we drove out, we saw tons of dairy farms. Both of us were very surprised and disappointed to see them, and we thought that they should be removed from the seashore immediately. There were lots of cows concentrated in very small areas. The cows had trampled the vegetation, which causes the soil to erode, and the water to get really muddy. The erosion was by far the worst near the cattle feeding areas. The cows had to be fenced in, and so you were restricted as to where you could go. Actually, you were restricted to the road because there were fences along each side. We were really surprised to see the cows because it is a National Seashore. The point looks like a regular dairy farm. We have spent a fair amount of time at the Cape Cod National Seashore, in Massachusetts, and it looks nothing like this part of Point Reyes. At the Cape, the surrounding area looks natural and it doesn't have any farming on it. We think that national seashores should be as natural as possible in order to preserve the land, plants, animals and water for future generations.

Since we have come back from the trip, we have learned more about why the cows are there. The issue is way more complicated than we thought. Ranches have been in operation since the early 1800s on the Point Reyes peninsula. It was a common landing place for Spanish explorers when Spain occupied California. Then American explorers came and started ranches on the point. These have been passed down from generation to generation for the past about 150 years! In 1962, Point Reyes was made a national seashore. The government

The beautiful beach at Point Reyes National Seashore. Laura and Jenna had fun sliding down the sand overhangs that you can see. They are caused by the tide eroding the sand away.

didn't want to kick the farmers off the land since they had been farming there for so long, so the Park Service decided to let them stay. Most of the ranches were purchased by the Park Service in the early 1970s, but the ranchers had the right to stay for 20 to 30 years. Many of the ranches are now leased by the ranchers for five years at a time. Also, as Dr. Kathy Tonnessen of the National Park Service explained to us, the only way that the national seashore could be formed was to allow the ranchers to stay. If Point Reyes hadn't been turned into a national seashore, it would have become a big suburb of San Francisco.

When we were at the point, we thought that the cows were causing a lot of pollution. But Dr. Tonnessen explained that people would have caused more pollution if Point Reyes had become a housing development. In fact, the estuaries in Point Reyes are some of the cleanest ones there are on the west coast! We are very glad that the government decided to allow the ranchers to keep working on their ranches in order to have Point Reyes become a national seashore.

When we finally reached the point, it was really foggy and cold. We could hardly see anything. That's the way it usually is at Point Reyes. There is a lighthouse that was built in 1870 and operated until 1975. Even with the lighthouse to warn the sailors of the rocks, there have been tons of shipwrecks in the area. There were so many shipwrecks that a lifesaving station was built in 1890 to try to save sailors who had their boats crash on the rocks. Eventually the station was taken over by the Coast Guard. The point and lighthouse were really fun to see even though it was foggy and cold.

There are many other animals besides the cows that call Point Reyes their home. Since Point Reyes is at the boundary between two different climates, there are many different plant species. There are many southern plants that reach their northern limit and northern plants that reach their southern limit right in Point Reyes. There are also some plant species that only grow in Point Reyes and nowhere else! In the national seashore there are lots of different kinds of habitat. These habitats include different kinds of forests, chaparral, grasslands, salt-water marshes, fresh-water marshes, estuaries, streams, lakes, beaches, rocky intertidal zones, and ocean. Because of the many different kinds of plants and habitat, many different animals live in Point Reyes. Tule elk were reintroduced to Point Reyes after being wiped out there. They did so well that

Tule elk, like this bull and cow, live at Point Reyes National Seashore. (Photo courtesy of National Park Service)

some of them had to be moved from the northern part of the seashore, where they had been released, to the wilderness area in the center of the seashore.

Because Point Reyes sticks out into the ocean, it's a great place for birds to stop on their migration north and south. There are so many different types of habitat that it makes the seashore a great place for birds to nest or spend the winter. We think it's pretty amazing that almost half of all the bird species in North America have been sighted here. That's over 470 species! There are four different estuaries in Point Reyes: Tomales Bay, Drake's Estero, Estero de Limantour, and Abbott's Lagoon. They are considered some of the best examples of west coast estuaries that are still ecologically intact. These estuaries have huge concentrations of ducks and other waterfowl as well as shorebirds, especially in the winter. Tomales Bay has tons of herring and oysters. Some of the streams in the seashore used to be really important spawning streams for steelhead trout and salmon. Both these fish spend part of their time in the ocean and spawn in freshwater streams. Most of the salmon and steelhead fish are gone now because of things like dams, over-fishing, grazing, logging, farming, and erosion. The Park Service hopes to try to restore the fish populations in the seashore.

Lassen Volcanic National Park

"When we tug at a single thing in nature, we find it attached to the rest of the world."

~*John Muir*

Before we went to Lassen Volcanic National Park, we didn't know anything about it, and we never dreamed it would be one of our favorite parks. It turned out to be a very beautiful, interesting park that we enjoyed very much. It has gorgeous meadows; fantastic hiking; a big, snowy mountain; geothermal features; and lots of other volcanic stuff.

On our way to Lassen, we stopped at this really neat store outside of Corning, California (which is near Redding). The store was called the Olive Pit, but it had everything from almonds to pickled zucchini to candied ginger! We spent a lot of time in the store escaping from the 104-degree heat and sampling many of their food products.

Luckily for us, Lassen is much cooler due to the high altitude. In much of the park, there was still snow while we were visiting! Some places were still snowed in! The main road through Lassen stays closed each year until they can clear all the snow off of it. Some years, though, that isn't until the middle of July! So, if you're going to the park early in the season, be sure to call in advance to make sure the road is open.

Lassen Peak still had lots of snow at the end of June.

Lassen Volcanic National Park is located in the Cascade Mountains, which is a mountain range of volcanoes. Lassen is the most southern of the volcanic peaks in the Cascades. The mountain range goes all the way up to Canada. About 50,000 years ago, Mount Tehama erupted at the site of what is now Lassen. As the lava poured from inside the volcano, a huge empty space was left in the middle of the mountain. The mountaintop collapsed down into the space. This is the same thing that happened to Crater Lake, the only difference being that some of the side of Mount Tehama collapsed also so the collapsed Mt. Tehama didn't have a rim around it. The rim is what allowed water to collect over thousands of years to form Crater Lake. So, no lake formed in the middle of Mt. Tehama, but some other volcanoes developed along its side. One of those volcanoes is Lassen Peak. There have been many different periods of volcanic activity in Lassen. About 300 years ago, the whole side of the mountain at Chaos Crags collapsed. It left a huge pile of rocks at the bottom of the slope. The rock pile is called Chaos Jumbles.

Lassen Peak became active again in 1914 and had lots of eruptions for about three years. On May 19th 1915, Lassen Peak had a huge eruption. There was still tons of snow and so when the lava erupted, it melted all the snow in its path. This caused a huge mud avalanche that wiped out an area about 450 m (1,500 ft) wide and about 4 km (2.5 mi) long. Three days later, a huge cloud of really hot gas and debris spewed out of the volcano and burned all the remaining vegetation. Now that area is called the Devastated Area and you can see it along the main road of the park.

There are four different kinds of volcanoes inside the park: composite, shield, volcanic dome, and cinder cone. A composite volcano is a made of layers of cinder and volcanic rock called andesite. Mt. Tehama was a composite volcano. A shield volcano, like the one in Lava Beds, has a very gradual slope because it is formed by overlapping layers of fluid lava. This type of volcano formed the plateau in the eastern part of the park. A volcanic dome is formed by very thick lava that only flows a short distance. Volcanic domes are rounded on the top and have very steep sides. A cinder cone has no lava. It is formed by loose hot material that is blasted out of the volcano. It is shaped like a cone: pointy at the top and round at the base.

Lassen Peak hasn't erupted since 1917, but we know there is still volcanic activity inside the mountain. We know this because there are hot springs, mud pots, boiling water and other geothermal features in the park. The active magma chamber is probably right under Bumpass Hell, which is where most of the hot springs are located. Devil's Kitchen probably results from sideways flow of really hot water from the area around the magma chamber.

Lassen Volcanic National Park was created for its volcanic geology. It's a geological national treasure, right up there with Yellowstone. In fact, it has the largest concentration of geothermal features west of Yellowstone National Park. There are many other really neat things about Lassen, but the big deal about it is the volcanic activity.

Lassen Peak is the highest peak in the park. Glaciers have changed it a lot and carved it. You can see evidence of past glacial activity, like glacial lakes and moraines. A moraine is a pile of rocks that is left behind when a glacier melts back up the mountain. Often a lake is formed behind the pile of rocks, and it is called a glacial lake.

The first day that we were in Lassen, Dad had to work. So we practiced our musical instruments in the park headquarters parking lot. We had lunch with Dad's work colleague, Tonnie. After Dad finished his work at the park headquarters, that left the rest of our stay strictly for exploring the park, which was also part of the work we had to do. Dad had to go out and look at the resources in the park that could be sensitive to being damaged by air pollution.

First, we went on a hike with Tonnie. We hiked about three miles through beautiful meadows and forests and over streams up to Devil's Kitchen. We had to drive up Warner Valley to the trailhead, and the trail passed right by a resort called Drakesbad Guest Ranch. It had a huge pool that was fed by a nearby hot spring, and it looked very inviting on that hot day.

We actually crossed over a trickling stream of hot water that flowed down toward the ranch, but we didn't touch it for fear of getting burned, not only from the heat of the water but also from the chemicals in the water. There is lots of wildlife around the area. We saw a marmot on the way up, and took lots of good pictures before it got scared and ran away. We also met a couple of hikers on the way back who had just seen a black bear around the meadow's edge half an hour earlier. Unfortunately, we were a

Yellowbelly Marmot

little too late to see it. When we passed through the forest, Mom said that she wished she could bottle up the wonderful smell and bring it home with her. We both agreed.

The meadows were Laura's favorite part of the hike because of the millions of butterflies that fluttered all around us. She especially liked the beautiful blue ones. Jenna loved them too. There were tons of different wildflowers and grasses in the meadows, and the scenery was beautiful. We could see a snowy mountain looming on the horizon. The meadow was expansive and extremely gorgeous. When we finally got to Devil's Kitchen, it was really neat. Devil's Kitchen is a geothermal area with tons of mud pots, fumaroles, vents, hot springs, and boiling water coming from the earth. There were many different colors, including blues, reds, browns, and greens. Minerals in the water cause these different colors. The only problem we had with the kitchen was that it smelled like rotten eggs from the sulfur. Yuck! We certainly didn't want to bottle up the smell of Devil's Kitchen and take it home with us! Unlike other geothermal areas we have been to, Devil's Kitchen is away from the roads and crowds. This made it kind of special, because we were the only ones there at the time.

The gorgeous meadows that we hiked through to get to Devil's Kitchen. In the background is a nice mountain that just completes the scene. If we had come about five minutes earlier, we might have seen the bear in the meadow!

On the way back from Devil's Kitchen, we took a side trail to Drake's Lake. We got part way up when we came to Hot Springs Creek, which was roaring like a river because of the melting snow. We had our lunch along the edge of the creek, but we decided that it was too dangerous to cross, so we turned back.

Then we took another trail to Dream Lake. It was more like a nightmare than a dream! It was disgusting. The whole lake was full of algae and not the least bit inviting. Then we continued on to Boiling Springs Lake. It was really cool - we mean hot! It is a huge geothermal lake, which is so hot it is practically boiling. It is probably the largest hot water lake in the world! The water is a greenish white color because of all the calcium and other minerals in it. Around the edge, there is a thin crust of minerals with small red pools filled with high iron content. We sat by a big tree and gazed at the bizarre lake for a few minutes. We even watched a stupid couple walk right past

Boiling Springs Lake at its most interesting. The lake is in Lassen Volcanic National Park, and it's called "Boiling Springs Lake" because its waters are so hot!

the warning signs and the do-not-signs right to the edge of the water. We HIGHLY discourage such action, as the water is boiling and the mineral crust is only a few inches thick! If you have any brains, you would not go on top of the mineral crust and you would stay a good distance from the water. There was a little path around the rim of the lake, which is an interesting walk.

When we came back from our hike, we were really hot. So, we drove to nearby Willow Lake. Laura, Jenna and Dad swam, while Mom and Tonnie watched. The water was really warm. Along the shore, there were tons of snow plants, which we thought were really interesting and pretty. They are strictly a bright red color with no green leaves at all. This is because they contain no chlorophyll, which is the green pigment in plant leaves. They don't have chlorophyll because they don't photosynthesize. Instead of making their own food from the sun's energy, they get it from decaying vegetation. Basically, they live on rot rather than sunshine.

Painted Dunes are streaked with red, orange, yellow, and brown colors, in addition to the dark grey of the volcanic cinders.

The next day, we went on an eight-mile hike through volcanic sand, which made the hike a lot harder than it would have been on regular ground. The trailhead left from Butte Lake and went alongside the Big Cinder Cone, Painted Dunes, and Fantastic Lava Flows. Dad wanted to hike up the Cinder Cone, but we refused because it was so hot. The trail continued past Painted Dunes, which looked like they were painted shades of red, orange, and yellow because of the oxidized iron content. After the dunes, the trail went past Fantastic Lava Flows and through a forest to Snag Lake. The lake was very beautiful, and not too cold. We ate our lunch on a nearby log and waded for a while. After lunch, Mom, Laura, Jenna, and Tonnie headed back while Dad took a quick dip. The return hike was really hot and dry, and it was a lot like walking on the moon because we were walking through volcanic cinders with very little vegetation around. We thought it was amazing that any plants survived those harsh conditions because of the extreme heat and dryness.

After our hike to Snag Lake we walked a short distance from the parking lot to Bathtub Lake. It is a small lake that warms up really quickly from the summer sun. The water was really warm and it was only the end of June! It wasn't very pretty, but it was a nice place to swim.

Lassen Volcanic National Park is known for its beautiful mountain lakes and hiking trails. When we were there, we were captivated by the beauty of these trails, and are already planning a return trip that would involve lots of hiking. A very high percentage of Lassen's high mountain lakes are really sensitive to being acidified by acid rain; they are the most sensitive lakes in the country. Not too far behind Lassen's lakes in this regard are the lakes of Sequoia, Kings Canyon, and Yosemite National Parks. Fortunately, the lakes in these parks have not been heavily damaged because they don't get high amounts of acid rain, but the Park Service is still concerned enough to study this problem. To determine how much the lake is damaged,

This is a nice example of a cinder cone that we passed on our hike to Snag Lake.

scientists have to take into account two things: how much acid rain the lake and its watershed receive, and how much buffering is provided by the rocks and soils in the watershed. Buffering is when the acids are neutralized so they are no longer acidic. If a lake gets too acidic, many forms of life that depend on the lake are no longer able to live there. Most of the acid rain in California is, believe it or not, from nitrogen pollution that comes from cars and trucks.

We stayed at a really nice campground called Manzanita Lake Campground. We had wonderful campfires in the evenings and roasted marshmallows. Dad insisted that Laura practice her oboe, so she went outside and began to play. Then two girls from the next campsite came over to hear her play. Their names were Kim and Erica and they were cousins traveling together from Maryland. They played the flute and the oboe (just like we do) so we had a lot in common. Right before we left, Laura gave them her address and she has been pen pals with Kim ever since. Throughout the whole trip she had been practicing her oboe to get ready for the junior symphony tryouts. They were taking place while we were on the trip, so she had to audition right when we got back. She made it. Yeah! Laura played the oboe and Jenna played the violin in the symphony throughout the school year and we both have really enjoyed it.

Interview

Name: Kathy Carlise
Position in the Park: Member of interpretive staff

Q. *What are your favorite places in the park?*
A. Manzanita Lake is nice for picnics and hanging around. Bumpass Hell is good for seeing geothermal things.

Q. *Are there any good bike trails in the park?*
A. No, bikes can only ride on the roads with cars.

Q. *When is the best time to come to the park?*
A. July and August.

Q. *Are there any really pretty scenic drives that you would recommend?*
A. The whole main drive is scenic.

Q. *The water is really hot at the geothermal areas. How hot is it?*
A. Some of the water gets up to 260 degrees F! The water isn't just hot, it also has a pH of 2 or 3! This is a strong acid and it can cause chemical burns.

Q. *So you have to be careful of the water. What else do you have to watch out for?*
A. The rocks on Lassen Peak Trail are sharp and can cut you like glass.

Lava Beds National Monument

"None of nature's landscapes are ugly so long as they are wild."
~John Muir

When we first arrived at Lava Beds National Monument, the overall consensus was that it was hot, dry, flat, and not very interesting. Boy were we wrong! It turned out to be one of our favorite parks. The best part about Lava Beds, as most everyone who visits the monument would agree, was the caves. They were just fantastic! When we first arrived, it was pretty late, so we didn't get to go on any guided tours through caves that day. We did go explore a little cave located right outside the visitor center called Mushpot Cave. It has a self-guided tour through a lighted lava tube cave that identified lots of things like lavacicles, mineral deposits, pull-offs, balconies, and other really interesting cave

Interview

Name: Loren Berlin
Position in the Park: SCA volunteer

Q. *What is you favorite hike in the monument?*
A. I like hiking Symbol Bridge, Schonchin Butte and Whitney Butte.

Q. *When is the best time to come to the monument?*
A. Winter.

Q. *What is your favorite cave?*
A. Valentine Cave.

Q. *What is your favorite thing about Lava Beds?*
A. I think this monument is a hidden treasure, because not many people come here and there are lots of things to do, if you really explore.

Q. *Where can you learn about the history of the monument?*
A. Captain Jack's Stronghold is the best place, but the petroglyphs are good too.

Q. *Where is the best bird watching?*
A. The wildlife refuge.

formations. It was a great way to experience a cave without taking a long hike. After visiting Mushpot Cave, we couldn't wait to see the others. Cave exploring, also called spelunking, is really fun. All the caves in Lava Beds are lava tubes, so they are very different from the caves in Pinnacles, Sequoia, and Kings Canyon. A lava tube cave is formed when the molten lava on top and on the sides of the flow cools and hardens while the lava below continues to flow on. This leaves an open tube in the middle with a rock ceiling, walls, and floor. In some places, there have been many flows, so the lava tubes crisscross, go on top of each other and flow together, causing very intricate patterns and complicated mazes.

Many of Lava Bed's caves are very important habitat for different bat species. Bats use the caves for hibernation and summer maternity roosts. The monument is especially important for the threatened Townsend's big-eared bat. The biggest threat to these bats is people disturbing them in their habitat. The monument is also home to the northern-most colony of Brazilian free-tailed bats.

The first night that we were at Lava Beds, we went to a talk and slide show at the campground about bats. Loren Berlin was the speaker. We thought she had some great slides of bats and she gave a very interesting presentation. She talked about how bats are really people's friends because they eat millions of mosquitoes. She also said that there are vampire bats, but not in the United States. All the bats in the United States eat insects. The bats that drink blood and the bats that eat fruit live in Central and South America.

June 28th

Today we interviewed Craig Dorman, the superintendent of Lava Beds. He was really nice and he spent a long time talking to us about the monument and giving us lots of good information and suggestions of caves that we should explore. When he found out that we had never been to Fern Cave, he arranged for a private tour just for us [and the other scientists that Dad was working with]*! The park rangers were all busy working, so we had a couple of hours until our tour began. Mr. Dorman suggested going to Skull Cave on the 2:00 PM tour led by Loren Berlin. We took his advice and drove up to the cave. It is a huge cave found by J. D. Howard, an early explorer of Lava Beds. I thought the cave was really neat. It got its name from some human and animal skulls that were found by J.D. Howard. I was extremely happy to find no skulls in the cave. It was really cold and down at the very bottom there was a floor of ice.*

Our Fern Cave tour, led by Chris Roundtree, was the highlight of our visit to Lava Beds, and was one of the highlights of the whole trip. We entered through a gated hole, down a ladder, and into a garden of ferns. The ferns were all clustered beneath the small hole in order to soak up the amount of sunlight needed for photosynthesis. The sunlight was so scarce that, at the exact point a shadow from a rock hit the ground, nothing grew. The reason they were in the cave at all was the amount of water available to them in there. There aren't any ferns up above the cave because it's too dry. We walked around the cave and Chris told us about rabbits that had fallen into the cave and starved in spite of the ferns growing there. He also told us other interesting stories. Then, he showed us the many pictographs on the walls. Some included suns, people, animals, and what seemed to be their favorite: small dots that run around all over the wall in different patterns.

~Laura

The authors interviewing Craig Dorman, superintendent of Lava Beds National Monument.

Interview

Name: Craig W. Dorman
Position in the Park: Superintendent

Q. *What is your favorite hike in the monument?*
A. I personally think we have some really great hikes but the best place to go is Fern Cave. It's out in the middle of nowhere until there's a hole in the ground. If you look at the walls, there are hundreds of thousands of Native American pictographs. This cave was like a cathedral to them.

(Continued on page 94)

Fern Cave was a very important religious site to the Modoc Native Americans. The area that is now Lava Beds National Monument was the center of the universe to the Modoc people, and Fern Cave was the center of the center of the universe. It was the primary place for them to go for their vision quests, which were really important to their religion. The pictographs are all that remain that help give us clues about their vision quests. We thought that it was amazing that such a lush garden of ferns could grow in the cave when up above there was very little plant life. The plants that actually grow on the ground above the cave are desert shrubs. It was just a magical place.

(Continued from page 93)

Q. *What is your favorite cave?*
A. Catacombs Cave.

Q. *When is the best time to go to the monument?*
A. June through early July is the best time to come to the park; July and August are really crowded.

Q. *Where can you bike ride in the monument?*
A. You can bike up and down the roads, but we don't allow bikes on trails.

Q. *Where can you go camping in the monument?*
A. There is only one campground, built by the CCC.

Q. *Where are the pretty drives in the monument?*
A. Medicine Lake Road is really pretty. Glass Mountain is really cool. It's a mountain made of glass!

An example of many of the pictographs on the walls of Fern Cave. They are like pieces of the puzzle that we need to put together in order to find out more about the life of the Modoc people. We found them very interesting and at the same time mind-boggling.

Q. *Are there any ranger-led hikes in the monument?*

A. Two every day, one at 9:00 and one at 2:00, but check with the Visitor Center. If you go on any of our hikes you should wear long pants and sturdy shoes.

Q. *How did they name all the caves?*

A. Each cave's name has something to do with the cave.

Q. *What kind of animals do you need to be cautious of in the monument?*

A. Scorpions, rattlesnakes, bobcats, mountain lions, deer and antelope.

Since the ancient Modoc people held this place with such reverence, we felt that it was important to treat it with respect. While we were down in the cave, we hardly talked, and when we did it was in whispers. The whole place was awe-inspiring and unlike any other place that any of us had ever been to. It's very difficult to express our feelings about this place on paper, but it was obvious to us that this was a really special place. We were very grateful that Mr. Dorman was so kind as to organize the trip for us, and that Mr. Roundtree took his time to show us the cave.

The day we left Lava Beds National Monument, we decided that we wanted to explore another cave before packing up and heading back to Oregon. We went into the visitors center around 9:00 AM when the hike up Schonchin Butte was supposed to leave, but no one showed up because it was too hot. The hike was supposed to be led by Yvonne McMillan, who works as a naturalist in the monument. We were talking to her about the different caves and she said that Catacombs Cave was her favorite. She asked us if we had seen it, and we told her that we hadn't. We had been thinking about visiting the beginning parts of it, but we didn't want to go in too far because we might get lost. She asked if we would like her to take us on a guided tour of the Catacombs Cave, and it took us a millisecond to decide that it would be really fun to go. So, off we went.

We thought that Catacombs Cave was fantastic! The tour was a real adventure. It was like the caves that you read about in books. It reminded us of what we thought the cave would look like that Tom Sawyer and Becky Thatcher explored during their picnic. Throughout the whole cave, there were billions of little passageways that twisted and turned and crossed each other like a maze. In some places you had to climb up and down steep cliffs and in others you had to crawl though small places. Often, there were two different passageways that would take us to the same place. We chose the crawl-on-our-stomach-

Laura, Jenna, Yvonne McMillan, and Mom checking out the mineral deposits in the roof of Catacombs Cave. Yvonne explained all about the cave and how it was formed.

way whenever we could. This made the tour a lot more interesting. ☺ Many people have been stuck or lost in the cave for hours. You could go around in circles without finding a way out. We would never go in there without at least two flashlights. Inside the cave there were tons of really neat lava formations. Some of our favorites were lavacicles, cave coral, pull-offs, and the little lava flow marks that tell you which way is headed uphill. The lava flow marks on the cave floor are little horizontal ridges that show which way the lava was flowing. The tops of the ridges direct you downwards, which means that you are heading further into the cave. This is really helpful for finding your way out. We thought that exploring the cave was one of the high points of our trip. As far as caves go, Catacombs Cave is one of the best. Our idea of what a cave should be like was perfectly represented by this cave. While Fern Cave was more of a spiritual experience, Catacombs was an adventure. We were really grateful that Yvonne took us on the tour. We learned a ton about caves from her and we had an excellent time doing it.

As we were driving out of the monument we were already planning a return trip. Our whole family thought that the caves were really neat and they definitely deserved some more exploring. We decided that not only did we want to come back in the summer, but also in the winter when the ice caves are open.

The authors explore one of the countless passageways in Catacombs Cave.

Lava Beds has the greatest concentration of lava tube caves in the lower 48 states. The caves range in size from really small to Catacombs Cave, which has about 2 km (7,000 ft) of surveyed passage. Some of the tubes are right at the surface and some go about 45 m (150 ft) deep. Don't be fooled by the heat above the ground. The caves are chilly and you need a sweatshirt or jacket to explore them.

The monument has lots of evidence of early human culture because people have lived there for over 10,000 years. The Modoc Native Americans were a hunter-gatherer tribe who lived in villages along the shores of Tule Lake. When the early European settlers arrived at what is now Lava Beds, there were lots of conflicts between the two cultures. All of the Modoc land was taken over and the people were forced to go to a reservation off their land and live with other tribes. The Modocs resisted that and a war resulted in the early 1870s between the Americans and the Modocs. Captain Jack was the Modoc leader. The Modocs hid in collapsed lava tubes and other lava formations near the shore of the lake. They defended their position for many months against the American Cavalry. The Modoc tribe was forced to surrender after the American Cavalry cut off their access to water. After that, the tribe was pretty much captured. The place that the Native Americans fought from was named Captain Jack's Stronghold. The stronghold is a maze of lava passages where it was really easy for the Modocs to hide and shoot at the cavalry. We spent some time exploring the stronghold that gave us a nice historical perspective of the surrounding area.

Much of Tule Lake was drained in later years to make room for agriculture. We think it was a big mistake to drain Tule Lake, because it, as well as nearby Lower Klamath Lake, is home to the largest concentration of ducks and geese in North America. Each spring and fall millions of migrating birds stop on these two lakes. Also, because of the large numbers of ducks and geese that spend the winter on those lakes, over 900 bald eagles winter on the shores of the lakes and use the ducks and geese as their food source.

Lava Beds is a volcanic park. There are 17 cinder cones, lots of lava flows, about 450 lava tube caves, and many caves that contain ice year round. Basically, the park is pretty flat because the volcano that erupted there was a shield volcano. It was huge but not very tall, so the lava flowed gradually down the hill. About three-fourths of the park is sagebrush vegetation, with some grassy areas scattered around. When you get up to the higher elevations (like on the cinder cones) there are some trees. Amazingly, there are two species of amphibians in the park, even though the closest standing water is 16 km (10 mi) away. There are frogs in some of the caves, and we even saw one in Fern Cave, as well as a rabbit skeleton.

Down by Tule Lake, there is a separate piece of land that is part of the monument, called Petroglyph Point. It is a cinder cone that formed under the ancient Lake Modoc. The action of the waves caused big chunks of rocks to fall into the lake, forming vertical cliffs. The Ancients (pre-Modoc people) used to paddle their canoes up to the side of the cliffs and carve the petroglyphs, resulting in the name Petroglyph Point. Now

Interview

Name: Yvonne McMillan
Position in the Monument: Interpretive Ranger

Q. *What is your favorite cave in Lava Beds?*
A. I definitely like Catacombs Cave the best. There are lots of other caves but to me it's the most adventurous.

Q. *What is your favorite hike in the monument?*
A. I like walking amid the pines to Eagle Nest Butte.

Q. *Is there a good place to see bats in the monument?*
A. Anywhere where there is a light and moths collect would be a good place to look. Hercules Leg and Catacombs Cave are places where you can see them occasionally. If you find one bat it's a male. Females gather in colonies.

Q. *Where is the best bird watching?*
A. The Petroglyphs are a great place.

that the lake has been drained, the point is far away from water and very windy and dusty. It has over 5,000 petroglyphs, which is the largest concentration of rock art in California. Unfortunately, people felt the need to put their own graffiti on the point, so there is a fence surrounding the ancient rock art. We enjoyed seeing all the petroglyphs but we were disappointed about how ugly the fence was and how difficult it was to really see the petroglyphs (the fence is about ten feet from the cliff). It looks kind of like a prison.

Q. *When is the best time to visit the park?*

A. The fall is prettier than the spring, because the spring is really rainy and wet. You can see Crystal Ice Cave from December 1 to March 31, but you can see the other ice caves year round. The summer gets pretty hot.

Q. *When do the ranger-led programs start?*

A. You have to come between Memorial Day and Labor Day to go on one of those. They aren't open any other time in the year.

Q. *Is there a ranger-led program for younger kids?*

A. Yes, there is one up to the lookout. Some kids complain about climbing to the top. The lookout is really nice. We have the Lava Beds Jr. Ranger Program up at the Visitors Center. There is also the Jr. Lookout Program that requires the walk up Schonchin Butte. You can earn a badge with both programs. You can do this only from mid-June to early September.

rater Lake National Park

"Everybody needs beauty as well as bread, places to play in and pray in, where nature may heal and give strength to body and soul alike."

~*John Muir*

Crater Lake National Park is a big park with lots of things to see and do while you are there. But, the biggest attraction of the park is Crater Lake itself. We also really enjoyed seeing all the snow and the rustic, old lodge.

The lake sits in the collapsed cone of a volcano. The volcano was called Mt. Mazama. It was a big volcano (about 3,650 m [12,000 ft] high), had lots of snow and glaciers on it, and was active off and on for hundreds of thousands of years. Almost 7,000 years ago, there was a huge eruption. Hot steam and pumice poured out of Mt. Mazama. There is still pumice from that eruption all over the Pacific Northwest. Pumice Desert, a little to the northwest of Crater Lake, has about 15 m (50 ft) of pumice lying on the ground. After the pumice erupted, a great big lava flow poured down the sides of the mountain. The mountain actually lost 15 cubic miles of volcanic material! Fifteen cubic miles is the same as a box five miles long, three miles wide, and one mile high! That's a lot of stuff to lose. Because the mountain had lost so much of its insides, all that was left of it was its shell. So, the mountain top collapsed into itself. It took a long time for the collapsed shell to cool off and when it finally did, it started to fill up with water from rain and melted snow. This water formed a lake, which is now about 580 m (1,900 ft) deep. That makes it the deepest lake in the United States and the seventh deepest in the world.

Crater Lake gets its water from rain and snow (but especially snow) that falls on it and the surrounding rim. There are also a few springs that contribute to the water level. The lake loses its water from evaporation and seepage. Seepage is when the water goes out through the rock on the bottom of the lake

Crater Lake and Wizard Island, a volcano within a volcano.

and then feeds other streams and springs further downhill. The lake's water level will stay about the same when the amount of precipitation is about the same as the amount of evaporation plus seepage. Even though the lake level doesn't noticeably change in any given year, it can change quite a bit over decades. You could think of it as the largest rain gauge in the country. During a dry period, the level goes down, and in a wet, snowy period it goes up. From 1890 to 1930, the lake level dropped about 4.5 m (15 ft), but it increased right back up again during the next 30 years.

If you visit the lake, you will notice the pretty island in the middle. This is called Wizard Island. It was formed after Mt. Mazama had collapsed and was in the process of forming a lake. At that time, a small cinder cone volcano erupted out in the lake and the cinder cone that resulted is now Wizard Island. So, it is a volcano within a volcano.

Crater Lake is just one of many Cascade Mountain volcanoes. They stretch from northern California to the Canadian border and are all about 160 km (100 miles) from the coast. This is because, when the Pacific Plate collides with the Continental Plate, it is forced to slide underneath. As the front edge of the Pacific Plate goes further inland underneath the Continental Plate, it has to go deeper and deeper. That means it gets hotter and hotter, and eventually begins to melt. All this melted molten rock builds up pressure while it looks for cracks in the surface where it can release the pressure. These cracks become volcanoes, and the volcanoes are the Cascade Mountains. All the major volcanoes in the Cascade Range are about 100 miles from the coast, because that is the distance inland where the plate is deep enough to melt.

Crater Lake is unique because of its vivid blue color. It gets this color from its great depth and scarcity of algae. It is easy for us to see why people call this beautiful lake the "Jewel of the Cascades". A really special thing about Crater Lake is the clarity of the water. You can see extremely deep into it, and it is considered one of the clearest lakes in the world. The way the water in most lakes can become clouded (scientists call this turbidity) is from inflowing streams that bring grit and dirt with them. Crater Lake doesn't have a main stream flowing into it, so the water remains very clear. It does sometimes get turbid for short periods though. One of the ways that can happen is from mudslides caused by large storms.

The Park Service is worried that in the future it won't be as clear because of acid rain. This is not because they're worried about the lake acidifying; it won't because it has lots of minerals dissolved in it to buffer the acids. They're worried because acid rain also contains nitrogen, which is a major fertilizer. If the lake gets large amounts of nitrogen, the algae might grow a lot more which would make the lake not as clear.

There are several hiking trails in the park. One includes the Pacific Crest Trail which goes right through it. There is also a great cross-country ski trail around the rim of the lake in the winter. If you want to do this trail, it's a really long way so you have to be a serious skier to go all the way around. It's a gorgeous trail, though, and it has nice views of the lake. If you want to hike in the park, you can go on the previously mentioned Pacific Crest Trail, or there are many other trails in the park around the rim of the lake. The lake is surrounded by lava cliffs that are between 150 m (500 ft) and 600 m (2,000 ft)

high, so you can't just walk up to the lake. If you really want to get your feet wet, there is one place on the north side where there's a trail that takes you down to a place called Cleetwood Cove. From this cove, you can take a boat ride around the lake, which gives you the option of stopping to explore Wizard Island. There are rangers on the boat who tell you all about what you are seeing.

You can go fishing at Wizard Island (lures only), and there are two kinds of fish that live there, kokanee and rainbow trout. Both these fish were stocked because the lake was naturally fishless. Kokanee are land-locked sockeye salmon. They feed on zooplankton and insects, but there isn't a lot of food for them and they are skinny. Kokanee are a schooling fish, especially when young. They live out in the middle of the lake, but when they are smolts (young, the equivalent of adolescent) they make a trip to the edge of the lake. Scientists believe that they do this because it is their natural instinct to go out of their fresh water home and go to the ocean like other salmon. Rainbow trout live along the edge and feed on benthos (which are insects who live on the bottom of the lake), insects that land on the surface of the lake, and young kokanee. They eat a lot of kokanee smolts that come into their territory, and some can be up to seven pounds! Sometimes they provide some of the best rainbow trout fishing in Oregon!

We visited Crater Lake Lodge while we were in the park. It is right on the edge of the rim overlooking the lake. It is a really neat old lodge, with big rooms and lots of exposed wood. A few years ago the Park Service thought it was a big safety hazard and they were going to tear it down. It really was dilapidated and falling apart. But the people who like to go there and have gone there for years were outraged by this proposal. They managed to convince Congress to provide enough money so the lodge could be saved. Instead of tearing it down, they rebuilt it and preserved it for future generations - including us! ☺

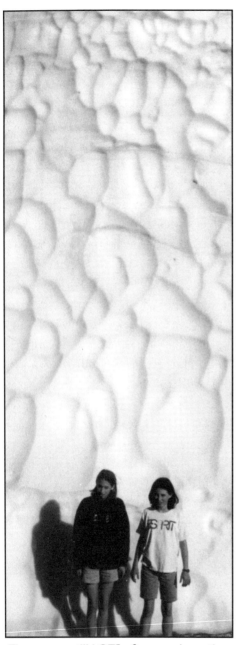

One of the things we liked a lot and were surprised by was the huge amount of snow still unmelted. Even though we were there at the end of June, there was still more than 6 m (20 ft) of snow in some places. Amazingly, in the average winter Crater Lake gets about 15 m (50 ft) of snow. In some winters, it gets way more! We had a lot of fun playing in the snow and having a huge family snowball fight. We let Mom and Dad think they were winning, until we forced them to retreat all the way back to the car where we pelted their windows with snowballs.

There was still LOTS of snow along the road up to Crater Lake. This is where we had our snowball fight.

Interview

Name: Gary Larson

Position: USGS biologist and Crater Lake researcher since
        1984

Q. *How did they figure out how deep Crater Lake is?*

A. Several ways. In the late 1800s they lowered a weight on a
   piano wire many times and did soundings. It was fairly
   accurate, but to be more accurate now they do an echo
   sounding or use SONAR. They send sound waves down
   there, and the time it takes for the sound to get to the
   bottom and back is related to the depth.

Q. *Is there a possibility of another Wizard Island?*

A. Any volcano in the Cascade Range could blow. There is
   another cone in the lake called Merriam Cone, but you
   can't see it because it doesn't breach the surface of the
   water. There's still thermal energy down there, and the
   magma chamber is still there.

Q. *What is your favorite thing to do in the area?*

A. My favorite thing to do is to go down to the lake and do my
   research and find out how it works. It is a real privilege to
   be part of the ecosystem there.

(Continued on page 110)

(Continued from page 109)

Q. *Wasn't the lake explored by a mini sub?*

A. Yes, it's a hydro sub called the Deep Rover. It is a one person sub with mechanical hands and cameras on board.

Q. *Are there osprey and eagle nests around the lake?*

A. I don't know of any osprey nests, but the last time we were there the lake surface looked like glass, but there was a storm coming and we were in an aluminum boat. So, we got off the lake fast and saw a bald eagle nest up in one of the trees along the lake shore. It was the first eagle nest seen for several decades!

Q. *Can you tell us about the research at Crater Lake that would be most interesting to kids?*

A. I'd say the color of the water is interesting to kids. It would be interesting to go to Wizard Island and learn about how it was formed. The fish and aquatic insects would probably be interesting. Also, you can see the weather buoy in the middle of the lake. I think the best thing for kids to do is to get down to the lake and feel it and really be a part of it.

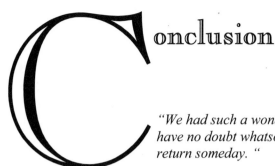

Conclusion

"We had such a wonderful time, we have no doubt whatsoever that we will return someday. "

~Laura and Jenna

In conclusion, we hope that you have enjoyed reading this book as much as we enjoyed writing it. It was a great adventure to go on this trip, and we sincerely hope that you will decide to take a similar trip yourselves. We highly recommend it. It took a long time and a lot of effort to write this book, but we have gotten immense satisfaction out of finishing it. We had a wonderful time on our trip from start to finish, and hope that we have included useful information that will help you on your travels.

National parks are beautiful places that need to be treasured and protected for the benefit of all. We hope to find every one of the special parks we personally visited in the same condition (or better!) when we return in the future. We had such a wonderful time, we have no doubt whatsoever that we will return someday.

Index

A

Abbott's Lagoon 76
acid rain 55, 85-86, 106
Ahwahnee Hotel 40
air pollution............ 26, 55-56, 80
art classes.................................32
Aster Lake.................................50

B

Balconies Cave 61-64, 67
Balconies Cliff..........................67
Bald Hills............................22, **23**
bat 64-65, 91, 100
Bathtub Lake............................85
beach..........17, 20, 22, 69, **74**, 75
bear 19, 41, 55-56, **56**, 58, 68, 81, **82**
bee......................................65-66
Big Tree...................................16
biking....23, 38-39, 59, 68, 87, 94
bird watching .22, 62, 69, 90, 100
Boiling Springs Lake 82, **83**
boiling water 80-81, 83
Bolinas Lagoon.........................71
buffering 55, 86, 106
Bumpass Hell.....................80, 87
Butte Lake................................84
butterfly 49, 81

C

Captain Jack's Stronghold .90, 99
Cascade Mountains ..78, 105, 109
Catacombs Cave....94, 96-97, **97-98**, 98, 100
cave......49, 52, 61-64, 66-67, 89-101, **95**, **97-98**
cave coral.................................97
Cedar Grove.............................58
Cedar Loop 58
Chalone Creek 62
Chaos Crags.............................79
Chaos Jumbles 79
chaparral 39, 64-66, 75

chlorophyll 83
cinder cone 79, **85**, 99, 105
Cleetwood Cove 107
Coast Miwok Native American Village 71
composite volcano.................. 79
Congress Trail 58
Continental Plate 105
Cottonwood Pass..................... 58
cow 73-75
Crater Lake...... 79, 103-106, **104**, 108-110, **108**
Crater Lake Lodge................. 107
Crescent Meadow.............. 54, 59
Crystal Cave 52
Curry Village.................... 35, 39

D

Devastated Area 79
Devil's Kitchen 80-81, **82**
Disneyland 57
Drake's Estero 76
Drake's Lake 82
Drakesbad Guest Ranch 80
Dream Lake.............................. 82

E

eagle 68, 99-100, 110
earthquake 63, 70, 72
Earthquake Trail...................... 70
East Pinnacles Campground.... 68
El Capitan......................26-27,40
elk............. **19**, 19-20, 75, **75**, **106**
Emerald Lake 58
erosion...17-18, 62, 72-73, **74**, 76
Estero de Limantour 76
estuary 69, 74-76
evaporation..................... 104-105

F

Fantastic Lava Flows............... 84
Fern Canyon 20-21, 29
Fern Cave 92-94, **95**, 97, 100
fire 51-52
fish.................... 18, 76, 107, 110

flower...22, 41, 44, 49, 62, 68, 81
fog drip 17
fumeroles 81

G
General Sherman tree 50-51
geothermal 77, 80-82, 87
Giant Forest 50, 52, 54
giant sequoia 35
glacial lake 80
glacier 26, 34, 44, 80, 103
Glacier Point.........35, **36**, 39, 55
Glass Mountain.......................94
Gold Bluffs Beach 20
Grant Grove 49
Grizzly Giant 35

H
Half Dome 26-27, 30, 35
Hercule's Leg.........................100
Hetch Hetchy 32, 35-36
hiking... 19-20, 22, 27, 29-30, 35,
    37-39, 41, 46-47, 50, 57-59, 61-
    62, 66-67, 70-71, 77, 80-81, **82**,
    84-85, 90, 93, 95, 100, 106
Howard, J.D............................92
hot springs.......................... 80-81
Hot Springs Creek...................82
House and Senate trees 51

I
ice cave 98-99, 101

J
Jedediah Smith State Park
    Campground...................18, 22

K
Kings Canyon 47, 58
Kule Loklo 71

L
Lassen Peak **78**, 79-80, 87
Lassen Peak Trail....................87
lava ... 78-79, 91, 97-99, 104, 106

lava tube cave 89, 91, 98-99
lavacicles 89, 97
lighthouse 75
Lodgepole Campground 57, 59
lodgepole pine 39, 50

M
Maggie....................................70
Manzanita Lake Campground 86-
    87
Mariposa Grove 35
marmot 49-50, **50**, 56, 81, **81**
Medicine Lake Road...............94
Merced River 26
migration 75, 99
Mineral King 58-59
Mirror Lake **29**, 30, 35, 37
mixed-conifer forest 39
Modoc 94, **95**, 96, 98-100
moraine...................................80
Morgan horse....................71, **72**
Morro Rock 54-55, **54**, 57-58
Mt. Tehama 78-79
Mt. Mazama....................103-105
Mt. Whitney............................58
mud pots 80-81
Muir, John . 25, 32-35, **42**, 42-46,
    58, 77, 89, 103
Mush Pot Cave 89, 91

N
Native American village...30, 32,
    71
nitrogen...........................86, 106
Nevada Falls 27, 35

O
Olive Pit.................................77

P
Pacific Crest Trail............58, 106
Pacific Plate..........................105
Painted Dunes...................84, **84**
Petroglyph Point 100
petroglyphs 90, 100-101

114

photosynthesis 16, **60**, 83, 92
pictographs 92-94, **95**
pika 56, **57**
pinnacles **62**, 62-63, 66-67
Prairie Creek Campground 18, 20
Prairie Creek State Park . ..18, **19**, 23
ponderosa pine 39, 52
pull-offs 89, 97
pumice 104
Pumice Desert 104

R

Rae Lakes Loop 58
redwood 15-20, **16**, 22-23, 50
rock climbing 40, 62, **63**
Roosevelt, Theodore 45, 62-63

S

San Andreas Fault 63, 70-72
San Joaquin Valley 44, 55
Schonchin Butte 90, 96, 101
scorpion **49**, 49, 68, 95
seepage 104-105
sequoia ...35, 45, **48**, 49-52, **51-52**, 54-55, **54**, 58
Sierras 33, 43-45, 56
Sierra Club **42**, 45-46, 59
shield volcano 79-99
skiing 37, 59, 106
Skull Cave 92
Smith River 18, 22-23
Smokey 70
Snag Lake 84-85, **85**
snow plant **60**, 83
spelunking 91
swimming ..18, 20, 23, 37, 61, 68, 70, 73, 85
Symbol Bridge 90

T

talus cave 61, **62**, 63, 66
tectonic plate 72
Tharp's Log 54, 58

Tokopah Falls 49-50, 58
Tomales Bay 71, 73, 76
Tule Lake 98-100
Tuolumne Meadows 40
turbidity 106

V

Valentine Cave 90
vents 81
Vernal Falls 27, **28**, 29-30, **31**, 35
vision quest 94
volcano 62, 77-80, 84, **84**, 99, 103-105, **104**
volcanic dome 79

W

Washburn Point 35
waterfall 21, 25-26, 29, 37, 50, 61
Wawona Campground 41
wild pigs 65, 67
Willow Lake 83
Wizard Island **104**, 105, 107, 109-110

Y

Yosemite Falls 26-27, 35, **36**
Yosemite Road Guide 38
Yosemite Valley 25-27, 32, 35, **36**, 37-39, 44
Yosemite Village 30, 32, 35

About the Authors

Jenna and Laura Sullivan are 8th and 9th grade students at Ashbrook Independent School and Corvallis High School, respectively, in Corvallis, Oregon. They both love sports, music, hiking, nature, and animals. They have spent a great deal of time exploring national parks throughout the western United States, accompanying their parents on scientific research and assessment projects. As a result, they have become experts on the parks in their own right. They enjoy science, writing, math, and history, and began publishing their own extended family "newspaper," called the *Puptown News*, when they were 6 and 7 years old.